Philip Carr-Gomm is a writer and psychologist living in Sussex. He is the author of *The Druid Way* and *Druidcraft*, and the co-author of *The Druid Animal Oracle* and editor of the *Book of Druidry*, *The Druid Renaissance* and *In the Grove of Druids*. In 1988 he was asked to lead The Order of Bards, Ovates and Druids, one of the largest international Druid groups. He combines his role as Chief Druid with a private practice in psychotherapy, writing and giving workshops worldwide. Since his first book appeared in 1991 he has been increasingly in demand worldwide for radio, television and newspaper interviews, and for lecturing. (A full listing can be found at his author's website at http://druidry.org/pcg)

DRUID MYSTERIES

ANCIENT WISDOM FOR THE 21ST CENTURY

PHILIP CARR-GOMM

RIDER

LONDON · SYDNEY · AUCKLAND · JOHANNESBURG

This book is dedicated to Nuinn
and to Charlotte, Sophia, Lawrence and Matthew

10 9 8 7 6 5 4 3 2 1

First published in 2002 by Rider,
an imprint of Ebury Press, Random House,
20 Vauxhall Bridge Road, London SW1V 2SA

Random House Australia (Pty) Limited
20 Alfred Street, Milsons Point, Sydney,
New South Wales 2061, Australia

Random House New Zealand Limited
18 Poland Road, Glenfield,
Auckland 10, New Zealand

Random House South Africa (Pty) Limited
Endulini, 5A Jubilee Road,
Parktown 2193, South Africa

The Random House Group Limited Reg. No. 954009

Papers used by Rider are natural, recyclable products
made from wood grown in sustainable forests.

Typeset by seagulls
Printed and bound by MacKays of Chatham plc, Kent

A CIP catalogue record for this book is available from the British Library

ISBN 0-7126-6110-7

CONTENTS

ACKNOWLEDGEMENTS

The core of this book was originally published in 1991 as *The Elements of the Druid Tradition*. Although *Druid Mysteries* is developed from this core, much material has been added, deleted or rewritten, so that it is almost a completely different book. More than a decade after the first book appeared, it became clear to me that a major revision was needed: Druidry as a way of life or spiritual practice had experienced such an extraordinary flowering and evolution since then, so much new material and scholarship had been published in this field, and I had learned so much more about the subject during this time.

The acknowledgements that I cited in the first book still apply. I am deeply grateful to the following friends, without whose inspiration or help I could not have written it: Stephanie Carr-Gomm, Douglas Lyne, Alice Wilcox, Susan Mears, Simon Seligman, Vera Chapman, Jay Ramsay, Michael Brookman, Glynn Morris, Chauncey Catto, Nicholas Spicer, Bede Johnson, Colin and Liz Murray, John and Caitlin Matthews, and the many members of the Order of Bards, Ovates and Druids whose promptings, gatherings, wisdom and encouragement led to its writing.

In addition, for this new version of the book, I would like to thank Ronald Hutton, whose comments as an historian have proved invaluable, Cairistiona Worthington for the inspired wording given in the excerpt from the Druid wedding ceremony, Sue Lascelles, whose perceptive suggestions as an editor have helped to make this a better book, and the management and residents of Spielplatz who provided such an idyllic atmosphere in which I could finish work on the manuscript.

CHAPTER ONE

THE HEART'S DREAM

The journey we begin as we answer the call is long,
and filled with all that we have been and all that we will become.
Cairistiona Worthington, *Druids – A Beginner's Guide*

Somewhere in everyone's heart there is a dream trying to be born. But when we look at the world around us it often seems as if collectively we have created a nightmare – we see appalling poverty and suffering, the devastation of terrorism, war and industrialisation. And yet we also find extraordinary beauty – we can walk into green valleys, climb hills that look out across forests and towards oceans, and we can close our eyes and feel the sun and the wind on our faces and bodies, and remember our dreams. For each of us those dreams will be different, and yet – deep down – I believe there is also a common dream, a hope shared by most of humanity, that our lives, and the lives of all beings, become filled with purpose and meaning, rich in experience and freedom, wisdom and creativity.

This book is about a way of life that can help us to find this universal dream in our hearts, and that can also help us to *live* it – so that, in however small a way, we can contribute to changing the world around us.

Thirty-five years ago, when I first heard about this way of life, I had no idea how important it would become to me, as it is to countless people the world over. My father worked as a teacher for a man who ran a private college in London, and who was also a Chief Druid. This intrigued me – how could anyone be a Druid, let alone a 'Chief Druid', in twentieth-century London? He invited me to attend a Druid ceremony, and at that moment began the long journey I have travelled ever since, and which eventually led to my taking on his role as leader of the Druid group he founded: the Order of Bards, Ovates and Druids.

Since that time, which seems so long ago now, Druidry (or Druidism, which means the same thing) has evolved to become one of the major 'alternative' spiritualities of the modern world. In this book we will explore the origins of Druidry in remote antiquity, and its modern manifestations – but all the time I shall be holding in mind two questions:

🌰 What is there of value in Druidism for the present-day?

🌰 How can we use the ideas of Druidism to benefit ourselves and make the world a better place?'

OPENING THE DOOR

The word 'Druid' provides us with our first key to answering these questions and to understanding the Druid Mysteries. It's as if the sign on the front door can tell us a great deal, if we will only pause to read it before trying to get the door open.

There are two kinds of words – connotative and denotative. When we go to the dentist or have surgery we hope they will use denotative words: 'Drill! Scalpel!' These are words that denote specific objects and everyone agrees about what they mean. When we listen to the lyrics of a song or the words of a poem, we hear connotative words – words that connote and hence evoke a host of associated ideas and images, sometimes smells and sounds and feelings too. Agreement isn't so necessary or so prevalent with connotative words.

'Druid' is such a word. Even without knowing its etymology it evokes images of wizards and sages, of Gandalf- or Merlin-like figures, ideas of ancient wisdom and arcane knowledge, and when we consider the various theories of the word's origin, it becomes even more evocative.

Some modern scholars agree with the classical Roman and Greek authors that the most likely derivation is from the Celtic word for oak – *dru* – combined with the Indo-European root *wid* – to know – giving their translation of the word Druid as 'One with knowledge of the oak' or 'Wise person of the oak'. Support for this derivation comes from the words for oak in Irish, Welsh and Greek:

Irish: *daur* (*drui* = druid)
Welsh: *derw* (*derwydd* = druid)
Greek: *drus* (*druidai* = druids)

Although it may at first sight seem odd that the Druids' knowledge should be limited to one tree, obviously the oak stands symbolically for all trees, since it was one of the oldest, most prevalent and most revered members of the forest. Those who possessed knowledge of the oak possessed knowledge of all the trees. Further support for the idea that the word Druid connects both knowledge and trees is found in the fact that in Irish trees are *fid* and knowledge *fios*, while in Welsh trees are *gwydd* and *gwyddon* is a 'knowledgeable one', from which we can suggest that the Druid was one with 'knowledge of the trees' or was indeed a 'forest sage'. The forest is synonymous with the wild, the sage embodies wisdom. Placed together, these two words suggest that Druidry offers us a path of 'wild wisdom'.

Further possible sources or influences upon the term Druid are: *draoi* – Gaelic for 'magician'; *dryad* – Greek for 'tree or wood 'nymph'; and *druaight* – Manx for 'enchantment'. Even though we cannot be sure whether these were etymologically involved in the creation of the term, they act as intriguing associations, giving us the image of a Druid as a 'knower of the tree-spirits, knower of magic, knower of enchantment'.

Other scholars suggest that the word is derived from the pre-Indo-European root *deru*, which means firm, solid, strong or steadfast, combined with the root *weid*, which means to see, creating a term that could translate as 'strong seer'.

To get a sense of how it might feel to be a Druid, try saying this: 'I am strong – a steadfast seer, a knower of magic and enchantment. I am a sage of the forest. I know the secrets of the oak and the wildwood.' Say it several times over, with as little inhibition and as much conviction as you can muster. It's important to say it out loud, because the voice has magical properties, which we shall explore soon when we look at the work of the Bards. If you're reading this in a public place, astonish those around you or wait till you get home!

If the exercise works for you, you will have experienced something of what it means to be a Druid – a man or a woman who even today can feel the pulse of life in the earth beneath them and the trees around them. Admittedly this is heady stuff, and we risk being seduced and deluded by the 'glamour' and romance of it all, but if we can keep our feet on the ground and try to be as sensible and as clear-seeing as we can, there exists the very real possibility that one day we will become knowers of magic and enchantment, and that we will be able to give birth to the dream in our hearts.

DRUIDS AND DRUIDESSES

Gaine daughter of pure Gumor,
nurse of mead-loving Mide,
surpassed all women though she was silent;
she was learned and a seer and a Druid.

(*The Metrical Dindsenchas*)

But why all this talk of only Druids? Where are the Druidesses? Some people think that Druidry is patriarchal, but this is not true. It is true that with the seventeenth- and eighteenth-century revival of interest in Druidism, groups were dominated by male members, but this is no longer the case, and today most Druid groups have equal numbers of women and men. Classical and Celtic accounts show that both male and female Druids existed, and Celtic laws offered greater privileges to women than most cultures of the time. Just as it is literally and politically correct to use such terms as actor and waiter when referring to either gender, so in this book the word Druid applies to either gender also.

DRUIDRY CELEBRATES LIFE, SEXUALITY, NATURE AND THE EARTH

Until recently Druidry was little understood by most people, and was hardly considered by scholars and historians. But over the last twenty years or so a great change has taken place. Druidry has moved from the very fringes of alternative spirituality to occupy a position almost on a par with the established religions, even though many within Druidry do not consider it a religion at all – preferring to see it as a philosophy and a way of life. Today you can send an email greetings card for a Druid festival from the BBC's religious programming website; Druids take part in interfaith conferences; people the world over practise Druidry, and there are books, magazines, websites and groups devoted to its study and pursuit.

The reason for this change is clear. As the twentieth century drew to a close more and more people became aware of the extent to which we were destroying the earth, and sought spiritual ways which reverenced the earth and nature. Druidry celebrates the natural world, and rather than focusing on how to transcend our physical existence, it focuses on celebrating our life on earth and on encouraging our creativity, helping the Bard within us to sing the song of our hearts and souls.

This focus on cherishing the earth and on encouraging our individual creativity means that Druidry appeals to many of those who are tired of the way conventional religions, both Western and

Eastern, can stifle individual joy and creativity with their focus on suffering, detachment and self-denial. Even when joy is offered it often seems only available through a person – a saviour or a guru – rather than through life itself and the astounding beauties of the natural world.

Druidry has an entirely different vision that celebrates and revels in life-as-it-is-now – not life as it might be in the hereafter or as it could be if we were able to break the cycle of death and rebirth. In addition, Druidry accepts and enjoys the means through which life comes into being – the inherently sexual nature of all life – and offers an approach that is based upon being fully involved in the world – on celebrating its beauties and joys, and on engaging its difficulties rather than trying to 'rise above them'. It suggests that we are *meant* to be here, not somewhere else.

A bardic story from Irish tradition of King Cormac's encounter with the sea-god Manannan mac Lir describes perfectly this type of sensuous spirituality. In the story, Cormac is shown a pool with five streams running from it. Manannan explains to Cormac that those who are wise drink from each of the five streams and from the pool itself, and that each of the streams represents one of the senses, while the pool represents Spirit – the deep centre within each of us.

Celebrating life, the body and its pleasures, as this story shows, does not mean sinking into a purely materialistic and hedonist lifestyle. The sensual spirituality of Druidry does not reject pleasure and surface beauty, but it doesn't reject Spirit and depth either. It is inclusive. A critic might say that such an approach leads to selfishness or indulgence, but in reality it leads to a far greater sense of responsibility – in particular for the environment. If, deep down, you feel your purpose is to escape being born on earth, or that humanity is fundamentally sinful and that you only 'pass through' here on your way to heaven, or possibly hell, then caring for the planet may well not be a priority for you.

Unlike the revealed religions that have scriptures which can then be argued and fought over, there are no sacred texts or even dogmas within Druidry. So in this book, for example, you will read of one approach to the subject, but it represents only one of many possible ways to understand a spirituality that is continually evolving. Each book and group expresses different ideas, and yet there are common themes and threads. One such theme is a deep love of the land, the earth that is our home. When it comes to love, modern Western culture focuses only on romantic erotic love, condemning all those who are not paired up in bliss to feelings of failure and unhappiness. Most, if not all, of those who follow Druidry as a spiritual path today see love in a much wider context.

In the Order of Bards, Ovates and Druids we believe that one of the central aims of Druidry today is to encourage us to broaden our understanding of love – so that we love widely and deeply. We see Druidry fostering:

Love of the Land, the Earth, the Wild
– with a reverence for Nature.

Love of Peace
Druids were traditionally peace-makers, and still are: each
ceremony begins with Peace to the Quarters, there is a
Druid's Peace Prayer, and Druids plant peace groves.

Love of Beauty
The Druid path cultivates the Bard, the artist within,
and fosters creativity.

Love of Justice
Druids were judges, and law-makers. Traditionally Druids
are interested in restorative, not punitive, justice.

Love of Story and Myth
Druidry recognises and uses the power of mythology and stories.

Love of History and Reverence for the Ancestors
Druidry recognises the forming power of the past.

Love of Trees
Druids today plant trees and sacred groves, and study tree lore.

Love of Stones
Druids today build stone circles,
collect stones and work with crystals.

Love of Truth
Druid philosophy is a quest for wisdom.

Love of Animals
Druidry sees animals as sacred, and teaches sacred animal lore.

Love of the Body
Druidry sees the body and sexuality as sacred.

Love of the Sun, Moon, Stars and Sky
Druid star lore, embodied in the old stories and in the stone
circles, teaches love for the Universe.

Love of Each Other
Druidry fosters the magic of relationship, of community.

Love of Life
Druidry encourages celebration and full commitment to life – it is
not a spirituality that wants us to escape from life

People are drawn to Druidry not only because they are looking for a
spirituality that cherishes the natural world – they might also be
fascinated by Celtic history, or by the old sacred sites, or by the old
stories. They might be drawn to it because of their ancestry, or
simply because it calls to them from the Otherworld or from the
world of memory. They may consider themselves Pagan or Christian
or Buddhist or of no particular faith, but all these approaches are
possible within Druidry, which seems able to become one's sole spiritual path or to enhance whatever path one is treading already.

Some groups follow the pattern reported by the classical authors of having three separate but related groupings of Bards, Ovates and Druids, while others just see themselves as a Druid group. Some people only call themselves Druids or Bards, or Ovates once they have been initiated and trained within a group, while others feel empowered to use these terms more liberally, and nowadays someone could well say 'I am a Druid' just as someone else might say 'I am a Christian' or 'I am a Hindu'.

Druidry can be practised alone or with others. Those who prefer the solitary approach sometimes call themselves 'Hedge Druids' just as some solitary Wiccans use the term 'Hedge Witch'. Others prefer to meet regularly within a local grove – a term which denotes not only a sacred clearing in the forest but also a group of Druids. A grove of Druids is similar to a coven of Witches or the congregation of a church.

A grove may meet in a member's house or garden, but more often than not they will try to meet out of doors – in a forest clearing or even a local park. In addition to celebrating the eight seasonal festivals described in a later chapter, they may come together to perform rites of passage when a grove member wants to name a child, or when members marry or die. Some groves will also meet regularly aside from these special times – perhaps once or twice a month. And at these grove meetings there may be initiations of new members, ceremonies enacted or teaching given. More often than not the meeting will become a social gathering – with impromptu story-telling and music-making, and with everyone bringing food and drink to share. To maintain a sense of safety and intimacy, grove meetings are private, but they are not secret in the way that a Masonic meeting, for example, is secret – taking place behind guarded doors and with special passwords and handshakes being needed to gain access. Druidry works with mysteries, not secrets. Just as love, when we try to understand it with our rational mind, is more of a mystery than a secret, so Druidry itself is a mystery that – like love – can reveal itself only slowly and with care.

The outer forms of Druid practice vary and are not mandatory – some groups wear robes, some do not. Some might hold separate grove meetings for each of the three grades of Bard, Ovate and

Druid, others not. Some might stick precisely to inherited rituals and ways of working, others might be more eclectic or experimental. Some might practise a combination of Druidry and Wicca – Druidcraft – and others might not. Groves can be made up of just a few members, or may number thirty or more, and although certain members will take responsibility for organising aspects of the grove's activities, no one person acts like a priest or high priestess.

It may seem incredible that a spirituality which can be practised in so many different ways – with such little conformity and so few overtly stated beliefs – can flourish. And yet it does. Part of the reason for this lies in the fact that Druidry is rooted in the imagery and inspiration of the natural world – it speaks of the mystery of life itself as it shows itself in the windswept sky, the gnarled oak, the sparkling wave. And another part of the reason lies in the fact that it is also a manifestation of the Western mystery tradition particularly suited to the world's needs today. It draws on the heritage not only of the pre-Christian Celtic world, but also upon the inspirations of Pythagoreanism, the Egyptian and classical mystery cults, the worlds of alchemy and hermetic magic and the work of countless writers and scholars. But it does this in a non-dogmatic way that honours each individual's unique needs and abilities.

Incredibly, miraculously almost, it manages to offer a philosophy, a spirituality, a way of life, a religion to some, that is also at the same time a living mystery school whose roots and inspiration we can trace far back into the distant past.

EXERCISE

Before we begin to explore these roots and the practice of Druidry, ask yourself which of the loves listed above calls to you the most. Try to do this spontaneously, without thinking so much that the rational mind gets in the way. Let your heart, your feelings and your intuition guide you as you read through the list again. The love or loves that have the strongest appeal may well show you the gateway through which you might want to approach Druidry.

CHAPTER TWO

THE SEVEN GIFTS OF DRUIDRY AND ITS ORIGINS IN THE WORLD OF TIME

It is often said – usually by those who have not studied the subject – that the worldview and philosophy of the old Druids is lost beyond recall . . . [but] it is by no means impossible to regain in the present age the spirit of original Druid philosophy. It is essential indeed to do so; for a revival of the old Druidic way of thought, acknowledging the sanctity of the living earth and all its creatures, seems the only alternative to planetary dissolution.

John Michell, *Stonehenge*

Today our biggest problem is that we have separated ourselves from Nature – so much so that there is a risk we may not survive as a species. We need philosophies, spiritualities, ideas that can help us get back in touch with nature again – our spirituality must become ecological. The Duke of Edinburgh, in a speech to a Washington conference on religion and ecology, controversially pointed to the direction in which we should look when he said: 'It is now apparent that the ecological pragmatism of the so-called pagan religions . . . was a great deal more realistic in terms of conservation ethics than the more intellectual monotheistic philosophies of the revealed religions.'[1]

It now seems that the Old Ways, reinterpreted for our times, can offer us the kind of spirituality that we need to heal the separation that has occurred between ourselves and our environment. Druidry is one such way, and although at first sight it might appear to be just an old curiosity, a quaint memory from the distant past, if we take the time to look at it more closely we will discover a treasure-chest just waiting to be opened. And in this chest we can find at least seven gifts that Druidry brings to our modern world:

The first gift is a philosophy which emphasises the sacredness of all life, and our part in the great web of creation. It cares passionately about the preservation and protection of the environment, and offers a worldview which is ecological, geocentric, pragmatic, idealistic, spiritual and romantic. It does not separate spirit and matter – it offers a sensuous spirituality that celebrates physical life.

The second gift puts us back in touch with nature with a set of practices that help us feel at one again with nature, our ancestors, our own bodies, and our sense of spirit, by working with plants, trees, animals, stones and ancestral stories. Eight seasonal celebrations help us attune to the natural cycle, and help us to structure our lives through the year, and to develop a sense of community with all living beings.

The third gift brings healing with practices that promote healing and rejuvenation, using spiritual and physical methods in a holistic way to promote health and longevity.

The fourth gift affirms our life as a journey with rites of passage: for the blessing and naming of children, for marriage, for death, and for other times of initiation, when it is helpful to mark our passage from one state to another ritually and symbolically.

The fifth gift opens us to other realities with techniques for exploring other states of consciousness, other realities, the Otherworld. Some of these are also used by other spiritual traditions, and include meditation, visualisation, shamanic journeying, and the use of ceremony, music, chanting and sweathouses, but they are all grounded in specifically Celtic and Druidic imagery and tradition.

The sixth gift develops our potential. Druidry as it is practised today offers a path of self-development that encourages our creative potential, our psychic and intuitive abilities, and fosters our intellectual and spiritual growth.

The seventh gift is the gift of magic. Druidry teaches the art of how we can open to the magic of being alive, the art of how we can bring ideas into manifestation and the art of journeying in quest of wisdom, healing and inspiration.

To begin our exploration of at least some of these gifts, let us look at where they come from. If you believe in the reality of the spiritual world, then it is easy to believe that the source of a spiritual tradition lies in that realm. Like a spring that emerges from an underground source, or a waterfall that cascades down a mountainside, a spiritual tradition enters into our limited world of time and space from another dimension – the Otherworld, as that spiritual realm that exists beyond the physical world is known in Druidry. It emerges from the timeless into time, and over the centuries different individuals and different groups of people have given expression to its guiding ideas.

THE LOST WORLD OF ATLANTIS

Some people believe that the historical origins of Druidry lie in the lost world of Atlantis. Recent writers have suggested that when the ice sheets melted as the last great Ice Age came to an end about 12,000 years ago many great cities, and perhaps even civilisations, were destroyed as the sea rose dramatically. More and more submerged ruins are being discovered around the world from that or later inundations, which suggests that the myth of Atlantis may not be a myth after all. This also offers a convincing explanation of the origins of the many flood stories that exist in different cultures.[2]

It has been considered unfashionable and overly romantic to believe that Druidry's roots lie in Atlantis, but if present discoveries continue we may find that this is a perfectly logical hypothesis. If global warming continues and sea levels rise, parts of the earth will again be submerged, but future generations will hopefully be less likely to dismiss the evidence of cultures and ideas that flourished in a submerged London, Paris or New York.

The founder of Anthroposophy,[3] Rudolf Steiner, believed in an Atlantean origin for Druidry, and he used his clairvoyant powers to observe the events surrounding the fall of Atlantis and the migration of its sages east and westwards. Eleanor Merry's *The Flaming Door* relates Steiner's discoveries of the origins of Druidism, explaining that the magicians of Atlantis had discovered the secrets of nature and worked in tune with her powers. But some used these same powers for their own ends – to dominate and manipulate others. In talking of the struggle between these two groups, Merry says, 'The War in Atlantis was the war of white against black magic – between those who saw in Nature the great Divine Mother of men and used her gifts for human welfare, and those who saw in Nature the satanic Temptress, offering dark dominion and cruel power.'[4]

As catastrophe struck Atlantis the 'baddies' were engulfed as they tried to hold on to their temporal powers. The 'goodies', having greater gifts of foreknowledge and a deeper conviction in the supremacy of spiritual wealth over the material, journeyed both east and west. In the west they landed on the shores of America, in the east, on the shores of Ireland and the western coasts of Britain.

Christine Hartley, drawing on the teachings of Dion Fortune's Society of the Inner Light, suggests in *The Western Mystery Tradition* that 'we, with our perhaps great inner knowledge, are content to take it that their [the Druids'] wisdom came with the basis of our mysteries from the great Temples of Atlantis'.[5]

If we accept this theory of the origin of the early Druids, we are able to understand more readily the reason behind the number of startling similarities that exist between Native American and Druid teachings and practice, including the use of sacred circles and sweat-lodges, the honouring of the cardinal directions, a belief in animal- and spirit-guides, the use of birds' feathers in ceremonial clothing and the adoption of specific animals as clan totems, or as personal or family names.

There is, however, no evidence that points to the origin of Druidry stemming from Atlantis in the early literature, though floods do figure in the Celtic tradition, and in the medieval Welsh collection known as *The Black Book of Camarthen*, for example, a maiden called Mererid uncovers 'the fountain of Venus' having been raped by Seithennin. The water from the fountain then covers the land.

There are stories of the submerged land of Lyonesse off the coast of Cornwall, and across the Channel in Brittany the story is told of the flooding of Ys. The king's wicked daughter worked bad magic and, taking from her father's neck the key of the dyke which protected Ys from the sea, succeeded in drowning both the kingdom and herself in the process.

These tales, and certain of the early Grail stories, speak of the same events that were supposed to have occurred in Atlantis – a violation of nature resulting in the welling-up of waters which inundate the land. The rape of the maiden Mererid, for example, can be seen as a mythic image for the rape of nature engaged upon by the evil magicians of Atlantis. The fact that the rape releases uncontrollable waters is symbolically fitting – for it is male analytical consciousness untamed by union with the Feminine that exploits the land, and it is the avenging power of the Feminine, symbolised by the waters, which is obliged to submerge the unheeding Masculine. And it is strange to note how history is apparently about to repeat itself in our age, with the waters of the melted ice-caps rising in response to our violation of the biosphere.

In another medieval work, known as the *Lebor Gabala Erenn* – The Book of the Taking of Ireland – which documents the mythical origins of the Irish, the biblical flood is documented, but Caitlin Matthews has suggested that in this story and others 'it is perhaps to some vague memory of Atlantis and the spring-guarding maiden that some of the stories look in their primeval vision'.[6]

Certainly Celtic tradition speaks of six races who arrived in Ireland from 'beyond the ninth wave' (the defined boundary of the land beyond which lay the neutral seas): the company of Cessair, the company of Partholon, the people of Nemed, the Fir Bolg, the Tuatha de Danaan and the Milesians. *Lebor Gabala Erenn* chronicles the invasions of these six races – attempting to integrate bardic memory with biblical tradition, making Cessair the grand-daughter of Noah. But it is the Tuatha de Danaan, the Children of Danu or Dana, the godlike race who have taken refuge in the hollow hills of the fairy-folk, the *Sidhe*, with the coming of the Milesians, who are taken by some writers to have been the Atlanteans themselves.

Those who favour the Atlantean origins of Druidry suggest that while some of the migrants from the 'shining lands' settled in Ireland and Britain, others continued to Asia and India – some by a northern route, others by a southern one. Later these migrants flowed back from east to west, and it is this later migration, they suggest, which has been chosen by certain 'exoteric' historians as the focus for their attentions on the origins of Druidry.

Leaving aside the Atlantean theory of origins, whose acceptance is a matter of individual judgement, we can now turn to the more conventional theories of the origins of the Druids, which are based on exoteric historical rather than esoteric or clairvoyant sources of information or speculation.

THE CLASSICAL ACCOUNTS OF THE DRUIDS

We know about the existence of the ancient Druids from the writings of the classical authors. The Druids were first mentioned in two separate works dating from about 200 BC and 400 BC respectively that have unfortunately been lost. In the third century AD Diogenes Laertius in the preface to his *Lives of the Philosophers* mentions that the Druids were discussed in a book by the Greek Sotion of Alexandria and in a treatise on magic, ascribed to Aristotle. (Historians are confident of the existence of Sotion's book, written in the second century BC, but believe the fourth-century BC work of Aristotle to be apocryphal.)

Taking a mythic or poetic view of the origins of Druidry, it is somehow fitting that we cannot be sure whether the earliest record of this tradition really existed, and that the second earliest record exists not in a library, but in the intangible world where only its memory is recorded over five hundred years after it was written. In this way our knowledge of Druidry rises slowly up out of the realm of the unknown, rather than bursting upon us in a flood of awareness.

THE FIRST WRITTEN ACCOUNT OF THE DRUIDS

The earliest extant record that we have of the Druids is that by Julius Caesar in the sixth book of his *Gallic War*, written about 52 BC. We then find a number of classical authors, including Cicero, Strabo, Diodorus Siculus, Lucan, Pliny and Tacitus, discussing the Druids up until about AD 385, when Ausonius wrote a collection of odes to the professors of Bordeaux which includes the story of an old man called Phoebicius, from the Breton stock of Druids, who managed to obtain a chair at Bordeaux university through his son's intervention.[7]

The work of the classical authors tells us something, though not everything, about what the Druids did and believed, and we shall examine some of this evidence when we look at the roles of the Bard, Ovate and Druid.

When Caesar wrote about the Druids he was describing a system that was well established and that had clearly been in existence for centuries. Sotion's book is dated to 200 BC and he was describing a group of spiritual leaders already in existence. By AD 600 Druidism had been totally eclipsed by Christianity. This gives us a span of 800 years in which organised Druidry flourished. It seems reasonable to say that when Sotion was writing the Druids could well have been in existence for at least 200 years, which gives us a time span of a thousand years, from the fourth century BC to the sixth century AD.

We can call this roughly calculated span a millennium of 'classical' Druidry – the Druidry we imagine when reading the classical accounts. Prior to that, we enter the era of proto-Druidry, which merges imperceptibly into the distant past and the age of pre-Druidry.

SOURCES OF THE CELTIC WORLD

In addition to the writings of the Greek and Roman authors, the other sources of written information that we have about the Druids come from Ireland, Wales and Scotland. But these are much later in date than the classical sources, and therefore present particular problems of their own when it comes to interpretation. The Irish texts date from the eighth century AD onwards, the Welsh texts were in the main only transcribed in medieval times, and the Scottish material remained in the oral tradition until the late nineteenth century, when folklorists began to document its treasures.

Although not committed to writing until the eighth century, the Irish texts are considered 'an extraordinary archaic fragment of European literature' reflecting 'an older world than any other vernacular literature in Western Europe'.[8] They mainly comprise hero-tales and summaries of law codes, and even though transcribed by Christian clerics, they are found to convey a reliable picture of the pre-Christian Druid world of Ireland that existed up until the introduction of Christianity in the fifth century AD.

The Welsh texts, like the Irish, are written versions of material that was originally transmitted orally. Transcribed much later than the Irish works, the Welsh corpus includes the *White Book of Rhydderch*, which was compiled in about 1300, and the *Red Book of Hergest* from about 1400. It is from the *Red Book* that the well-known tales of the *Mabinogion* have been extracted, and a part of this series of tales is also found in the *White Book* – the evidence showing that they were originally committed to writing between 1100 and 1250. Another significant Welsh manuscript, which conveys much of the Druid wisdom to us today, is the *Book of Taliesin*. This is of even later date, being thirteenth or fourteenth century, although some trace its origins back to the sixth century or earlier.

A further source of knowledge about the Druids and their work comes to us from the Irish and Welsh Triads, which are pithy wisdom-sayings based originally on Druid lore, and which have been gathered from many manuscript sources. From these and other texts we are given an insight into the complex syllabus of bardic training, and through their terse form we can glimpse the depth of bardic and Druidic thought. In addition, a study of the old Irish laws, known as the Brehon laws, gives us an extraordinary glimpse into the world of pre-Christian Ireland, even though they were not set down in writing until the sixth century – after the time of Saint Patrick. Since the Druids were known as the lawgivers, we can still hear today – across two millennia – the voices of these ancient sages whose ethical system was in many respects more humane than that of the dispensation which succeeded it.

Turning to the Scottish material, it might be thought that this would hardly be reliable as a source of information on the Druids, having been transcribed only in the late nineteenth and early twentieth centuries. But this material, which includes the massive collection made by Alexander Carmichael, published in six volumes between 1900 and 1961 and entitled *Carmina Gadelica*, serves only to substantiate the understanding of our pre-Christian heritage obtained from the earlier classical, Irish and Welsh sources. It also bears living witness to the extraordinary ability of cultural and spiritual traditions to survive for thousands of years being passed only from mouth to ear.[9]

It is true that all these sources of information at our disposal have been influenced, some might say corrupted, en route to the present day. Copying errors, together with sins of omission and commission, no doubt prompted by the Christianity of the copyists, may well have changed the material over time. The Welsh material in particular was subject to the influences of the troubadour tradition, of which the Welsh story-tellers formed a part, and it has been subjected too to corruption by the forgeries of a stonemason by the name of Iolo Morganwg.

Despite these changes, it can still be stated that the corpus of material which we have at our disposal for an understanding of Druidry is vast indeed, and to this day its riches have yet to be fully researched and appreciated. Even now only about a quarter of the Celtic texts that deal with the subject of pre-Christian Celtic spirituality and Druidry have been translated into English.

CLUES IN WOOD AND STONE

Our knowledge of the 'classical' period of Druidry can be supplemented, to a small extent, by a study of inscriptions, carving and sculpture. The epigraphic evidence available to us consists of some 360 inscriptions in what has become known as the tree-language of the Druids, Ogham, found chiefly on memorial stones in the south-west of Ireland and Wales, dating from the fifth and sixth centuries AD, and hundreds of dedicatory inscriptions, mainly found in Gaul, to Celtic gods or goddesses, although these date almost exclusively from the time when Britain and Gaul formed part of the Roman Empire.[10]

The iconographic evidence consists of sculptures and carvings, in both wood and stone, of human and animal forms dating from the sixth century BC. These two sources of evidence, in words and images, the epigraphic and the iconographic, become illuminating when set within the context provided for us by the textual evidence supported by the findings of archaeology, language studies and comparative mythology.

In coming to these sources of evidence we are presented with a rich and exciting field of study which in recent years or so has helped us form a picture of Druidry which suggests a continuity of tradition from the Neolithic right through to the Celtic era.

A CONTINUITY WITH THE STONE AGE – THE MEGALITHIC BUILDERS AS PROTO-DRUIDS

Neolithic farming communities dated to 4500 BC have been traced in southern Britain and Ireland, and as far north as the Orkneys to 3500 BC. It was these 'Stone-Age' communities who were the megalith builders and who erected their numerous stone monuments during the course of about two and a half thousand years, from 3500 to 1000 BC.

Those of us who envisaged our Stone-Age ancestors as 'rude savages' have been forced radically to alter our understanding of them in the light of discoveries pioneered initially by Sir Norman Lockyer at the beginning of the last century, but only fully developed in recent years with the detailed surveying and computing work of Professors Thom and Hawkins. This work suggests that the stone circles and other monuments of the Neolithic people were erected with an astonishingly sophisticated use of mathematics, which reveals our enlightened ancestors to have been in possession of an understanding of 'Pythagorean' mathematics over a thousand years before Pythagoras was born.

Megalithic remains in the form of burial mounds, standing stones and stone circles have been found all over the world – in Tibet, China, Korea and Japan, in the Pacific islands, Malaya and Borneo, in Madagascar, India, Pakistan and Ethiopia, in the Middle and Near-East, in Africa and the Americas. Owing to their similarities of construction, it has been tempting to suggest that these megalith builders originated in one or another place, and that the spread of these sites is due to their migrations. In reality, it is unnecessary to invoke migration theories to explain their ubiquity. The most convincing explanation for their worldwide distribution is found by looking at the theories of both archaeology and analytical psychology.

Current archaeology suggests that these monuments are similar all over the world because they represent the very simplest of designs – single upright stones, or several uprights supporting a horizontal, as in dolmens and burial chambers. The analytical psychology pioneered by C. G. Jung suggests that our own individual consciousness is embedded in a collective unconscious which results in similar manifestations of the collective human psyche occurring in widely separated parts of the world – no physical connections are required for similar artistic, cultural, religious or architectural phenomena to appear in different regions.

What is known for sure, however, is that the megalithic monuments of western Europe are among the oldest in the world. Carbon-14 dating places the majority of them between the fifth and second millennium BC. Since they are older than the monuments of Africa or Asia, the Near or Middle East they cannot have been 'seeded' from the south or east. Jean-Pierre Mohen says: 'The discovery of this early time scale (in Europe) poses in new terms the question of the genesis of these monuments: we must envisage a local origin for each of the main groups – Iberian, Breton, Irish and Scandinavian.'[11]

Historians used to believe the Druids could not have built the stone monuments because the Druids were Celtic according to the classical reports, and the Celts had not arrived in Britain at this early age. However, as we shall soon see, this opinion has started to change and it is now acceptable to call the Neolithic megalith builders of Britain proto-Druids, which distinguishes them from the Druids known to us from the classical texts. (The term 'proto-Druid' simply means 'early Druid', the prefix 'proto' meaning 'first-formed' or 'ancestral'.)

This primal, ancestral Druidry took a major step forward in its development when it merged or interacted with the traditions and beliefs of incoming peoples who have been termed 'proto-Celts'. The origins of the Celts themselves, however, are as difficult to determine and as prone to academic disagreement as are the origins of the Druids.

THE ORIGINS OF THE CELTS

Even using the term 'Celt' is fraught with difficulties. Colin
Renfrew, Professor of Archaeology at Cambridge, has identified at
least eight senses in which the term is used. Renfrew concludes with
'the strong suspicion that the term "Celts" is not a proper ethnic
term . . . but was imposed on a wide variety of barbarian tribes by
classical geographers.'[12]

It is important to understand that Renfrew does not deny 'that
there was indeed a language group, which since the eighteenth
century has been termed "Celtic", nor that there are significant
archaeological observations to be made about the material culture
and way of life at the relevant places and times'. But he stresses that
'these different and valid perceptions should not be confused by
lumping them all together as "Celtic"'.

The forebears of the Celts were probably the Beaker folk, who
originated either in central Europe or Iberia in the third millennium
BC, and the Battle-Axe folk, who almost certainly originated in the
steppe-lands of southern Russia at about the same time. The fusion
of these folk in central Europe in about the second millennium BC
resulted in successive cultures known as Unetice, Tumulus and
Urnfield. Some scholars argue that towards the close of the second
millennium BC the Urnfield culture becomes identifiable as 'proto-
Celtic'. From about 700 BC some of the descendants of the Urnfield
people have been labelled the Hallstatt culture, which can safely be
regarded as fully Celtic, as opposed to proto-Celtic. The Hallstatt
culture is traced for only 200 years, before it gives way to the La
Tène culture, which survived until the coming of the Romans.

If just the Hallstatt and La Tène type of cultures are regarded
as Celtic then the Celts only make their appearance in Britain from
about 500 BC. But if we see the ancestors of the Celts as the Beaker
and Battle-Axe folk, and term them proto-Celtic as some scholars
do, then we can trace the coming of proto-Celts to Britain at least
as early as 2000 BC, since Beaker sites in Britain have been identified from about this time.

Professor Renfrew argues against this theory, claiming that
although it is favoured by continental archaeologists, 'most

[British] archaeologists do not now think in terms of beaker-bearing immigrants on any scale'. Instead Renfrew, drawing on studies of historical linguistics, favours a theory of Indo-European origins, which was originally popular in the nineteenth century, but which – with revised underpinnings – he re-presents. He suggests that before about 6000 BC in the eastern part of Anatolia (now Turkey) people speaking languages ancestral to all the Indo-European languages were to be found, and that by 4000 BC some of these earliest Indo-European speakers would have reached Europe and possibly Britain.

The Celts are seen as originating from these Indo-Europeans. From the sixth millennium BC onwards they expanded from their homelands both eastward and westward, reaching Britain and Ireland in the west, and India in the east.

Studies in comparative mythology show us that Sanskrit literature documents ancient Indian rituals which are similar to those traceable in Celtic Ireland, and there are certain striking parallels which can be drawn between some Hindu deities and Celtic gods, such as the goddesses Danu of India and Dana of Ireland. Further similarities can be traced among the religious traditions of the Indo-Europeans, which help to give us a picture of Druidic practice that can be said to reach back in its origins to the very beginnings of Indo-European culture before 6000 BC. These similarities relate to the sanctity and importance of water; the probable offering of sacrifices; the religious symbolism of weapons; the use in some areas of circular and spiral motifs in religious art; a concern for calendrical and probably astrological observation; the sanctity of fire; and the sacred nature of the number three.

In many ways, the functions and conduct of the learned and privileged classes of Bard, Ovate and Druid were so similar to that of the Brahmin caste in India, that one scholar has suggested that an account of them reads almost like 'a chapter in the history of India under another name'.[13]

DRAVIDIAN DRUIDS

My old Druid teacher, Ross Nichols, believed the Druids may well have originated at an even earlier time – amongst a group of pre Indo-European peoples in India known as the Dravidians. These people were Jains. Jainism is one of the oldest religions in the world, and Ross once wrote: 'Of the known cultural communities it is the Jains who seem most like a society from which Druidry could have originated . . . The origins of Druidic traditions go back to a past remote indeed, almost as far back as civilisation itself, and at least into Neolithic times. There are links with Aryan and early Hindu culture and what is now the witch cult: reverence for both sun and moon, fivefold and threefold bases of teaching, circular dancing as worship, burning of the dead, the cult of certain animals, the existence of a priest-ruler caste, transmission of teaching by long memorised poems.'[14]

It should be noted that although some scholars have seen links between the Dravidians and the Druids, both the Druidism reported by the classical authors and its modern manifestations seem to bear little resemblance to Jainism past or present. When looking so far into the distant past, whether we are examining the theories of Ross Nichols, Colin Renfrew or anyone else, we will probably never be sure that we have found the truth.

A BALANCED VIEW

Historians used to claim that the Celts came to Britain in a series of invasions from about 500 BC, and that the Druids, being Celts, could not therefore have built the stone circles. The antiquarians of the seventeenth- and eighteenth-century Druid Revival and the modern Druid orders who claimed that the Druids built such places as Stonehenge were scorned by academics who believed that the completion of the stone circles antedated the arrival of the Celts by over five hundred years.

The evidence available to us now, however, suggests the revival and modern Druids are right about their ancient forebears, whether we consider the proto-Celts (and hence the proto-Druids) to have emerged in Britain in around 2000 BC, as Beaker folk, or even earlier as Indo-Europeans, as Colin Renfrew argues.

A balanced view of the evidence suggests that Druidry is best conceived as a tradition, a set of beliefs and practices, whose roots lie both in the Indo-European ancestors of the Celts and in the native megalithic culture. Both undoubtedly carried with them a formidable corpus of mathematical, astronomical, engineering and philosophical knowledge which fused together in Ireland and Britain, and probably only subsequently in Gaul, to form the powerful and multi-faceted group of Bards, Ovates and Druids that are referred to in the classical texts.

Whether we believe Druidry's origins lie in the spiritual world, in the temples of Atlantis, the rites of the Dravidians, or the gradual merging of Indo-European and Stone-Age cultures in western Europe, we can be sure that its roots stretch far and deep.

EXERCISE

After reading this chapter, spend a few moments forgetting all that you have read, make yourself comfortable, and allow yourself to come to a sense of inner centredness and calm. For meditation you can be seated cross-legged on the floor or in the usual upright sitting position on a chair. Some Western esoteric teachings state that to sit cross-legged on the ground is an Eastern posture inappropriate for Western meditation. This is incorrect. The cross-legged position is depicted in Celtic art and is therefore not exclusively 'Eastern'. It provides a sense of humility, of being in touch with the earth, and of being well grounded. Many people, however, find it difficult to meditate in this position, and prefer to be seated in a chair.

Close your eyes and feel all your concerns falling away from you. Often, in Druid ceremonies, having entered the circle, we begin by saying, 'Let all disturbing thoughts be laid aside'. Focus for a little while on your breathing, and then become aware of the sun rising. You might do this by imagining you are on a hillside or mountain top gazing at the horizon. Or you might feel a sun rising in your heart, or your solar plexus or in an internal way that cannot be described in words.

Bathe in the light and warmth of the sun for as long as you like. Then become aware of being fully yourself again. Feel full of vitality and strength. Become conscious of your physical body and surroundings, and when you feel ready, open your eyes. Do not stand up quickly – stretch a little before standing up or continuing with the next chapter.

CHAPTER THREE

THE BRIDGE OF A THOUSAND YEARS:

HOW DRUIDRY SURVIVED THE COMING OF CHRISTIANITY

To view nature as imbued with soul, and each creature
in the universe as alive and communicative, is a form
of animism consistent with the earliest spiritual framework
of the ancient Celts. But it has survived into
Christian and even post-Christian times.

Tom Cowan, *Fire in the Head – Shamanism and the Celtic Spirit*

During its likely beginnings in Neolithic times, Druidry was probably at first animistic and shamanistic in nature, until gradually it evolved into its three separate streams of Bardic, Ovate and Druid practice described by the classical authors. This period of sophisticated, even complex, spiritual practice continued probably for at least a thousand years before being eclipsed by the arrival of Christianity. During this time, from around the fourth century BC to the sixth century AD, Druidry may well have received influences from the Egyptian and Greek civilisations, for sages and philosophers throughout the ages have always undertaken pilgrimages and journeys to exchange ideas and knowledge. Certainly the Romans brought their influence to bear upon local indigenous spiritualities, including Druidry, and in addition it is said that legionnaires brought with them ideas and practices from the Mithraic mysteries of Persia to Britain.

Support for the view that the doctrines of the ancient Druids of this 'classical' period were influenced by the Egyptian, Greek and also the Orphic mysteries comes from tantalisingly brief statements of the classical authors who suggest that the Druids embraced the doctrines of Pythagoras. Pythagoras, who lived during the sixth century BC, claimed initiation into all the Greek mysteries and to have studied in Egypt. He founded an initiatory society, which accepted women and men equally, in Krotone (now Crotone in Italy). There he taught esoteric doctrines relating to the progress of the soul, reincarnation, music and mathematics. His doctrines seem to have been influenced not only by the Greek and Egyptian mystery schools, but also by the Orphic mysteries and by Thracian shamanism, possibly learned from his Thracian slave, who later – it is said – taught the Druids. Pythagoreanism has had a powerful influence on Western culture and spirituality: a neo-Pythagorean revival began in the first century BC which profoundly influenced gnosticism, hermetism and alchemy and evolved into the neo-Platonism of the third century AD.

Diodorus Siculus as early as 21 BC wrote that 'the Pythagorean doctrine prevails among them [the Gauls, whose philosophers, he states, were the Druids] teaching that the souls of men are immortal and live again for a fixed number of years inhabited in another body'. Hippolytus in the second century AD wrote 'The Keltic Druids applied themselves thoroughly to the Pythagorean philosophy, being urged to this pursuit by Zamolxis, the slave of Pythagoras, a Thracian by birth, who came to those parts after the death of Pythagoras, and gave them the opportunity of studying the system. And the Kelts believe in their Druids as seers and prophets because they can foretell certain events by the Pythagorean reckoning and calculations.' Ammianus Marcellinus in the fourth century AD called the Druids 'members of the intimate fellowship of the Pythagorean faith'. By this time mendicant Pythagorean ascetics were roaming the Greek-speaking world teaching their founder's doctrines. Caesar had recorded over four hundred years previously that the Druids spoke and wrote in Greek, and it seems quite plausible that there was contact between Pythagoreans and Druids at various times during the period of classical Druidry. Nevertheless, some scholars believe there was no Pythagorean influence on Druid doctrines, and that the classical accounts are flawed. In addition, Clement of Alexandria in the second century AD succeeded in confusing the picture by claiming that Pythagoras had learned his doctrines from the Druids rather than vice versa.[15]

However much Druidry was informed by the influences of Greece, Thrace and Egypt through the agency of Pythagoras or his followers, by the sixth century AD it had apparently ceased to exist. Whereas the occupying Romans had tolerated local religious practices in their vast empire, the new faith of Christianity would accept no rivals. Many people still believe that Druidry simply died out with the triumph of Christianity in Europe, while other people who have heard of the seventeenth- and eighteenth-century revival of interest in Druidism, often known as the period of 'romantic revival', ask, 'Isn't modern-day Druidry just an invention of the Romantics?' As we shall see, though there has been much invention over the years, the tradition did not die and the wisdom was not lost. One of the main reasons for this lay in the fact that the Bards were accepted within the new Christian dispensation, while their tales, which conveyed so much of Druid wisdom were recorded by Christian clerics. This enabled the golden thread of the essential Druid mysteries to be passed on to our own age.

THE BARDIC COLLEGES

Far from being outlawed with the coming of Christianity, the bardic schools continued to function in Ireland up until the seventeenth century, and in Scotland to the beginning of the eighteenth century. Professor Stuart Piggott, writing of one of the key moments of the revival period when a Druid ceremony convened by Welshman Iolo Morganwg was held atop London's Primrose Hill in 1792, states that the eighteenth-century Welsh bards, 'even if somewhat fallen on evil days by 1792, were not nonsense. In the Middle Ages, as with their counterparts in Ireland, they had formed part of the traditional Celtic hierarchy with genuine roots in the ancient past of the Celts and Druids.'[16]

That such a continuity of tradition should exist is impressive, and there are still other ways that show us how Druidry survived the long journey of over a thousand years from the sixth to the seventeenth and eighteenth centuries.

CHRISTIANITY CONTRIBUTES TO DRUIDRY'S SURVIVAL

Although Christianity ostensibly superseded Druidry, in reality it contributed to its survival, and ultimately to its revival after more than a millennium of obscurity. It did this in at least four ways: it continued to make use of certain old sacred sites, such as holy wells; it adopted the festivals and the associated folklore of the pagan calendar; it recorded the tales of the Bards, which encoded the oral teachings of the Druids; and it allowed some of the old gods to live in the memory of the people by co-opting them into the Church as saints. That Christianity provided the vehicle for Druidry's survival is ironic, since the Church quite clearly did not intend this to be the case.

Long before the Romans withdrew from their occupation of Britain in AD 410, Christian missionaries had come to its shores. Over the next three hundred years the population of the rest of the British Isles gradually converted to the new faith, which persecuted the old religion of the Druids with as much vigour as it dealt with any rival faith. The Druids in their turn were determined in their opposition to the new religion. Two of the Druids, in the king's court at Tara in Ireland, prophesied 'that a new way of life was about to arrive from overseas, with an unheard-of and burdensome teaching, which would overthrow kingdoms, kill kings who resisted it, banish all the works of their magic craft, and reign forever'.[17]

Some believe that the Druids co-operated with the Christians when they arrived in Britain, but this seems to be a myth. In the eleventh and twelfth centuries, Christian clerics in Ireland fell in love with their pagan past and tried to paint a picture of a harmonious integration of Druidry and Christianity. But the earlier Christian writers of the seventh and eighth centuries describe Christianity and Druidry as highly antagonistic to each other. In the 1930s the writer Eleanor Merry cited a quotation supposedly from the sixth-century Bard Taliesin, in which he says: 'Christ, the Word from the beginning, was from the beginning our Teacher, and we never lost his teaching. Christianity in Asia was a new thing, but there never was a time when the Druids of Britain held not its doctrines.'[18] Ever since then, this quotation has been used as proof that the Druids had similar ideas to the Christians and that, by extension, when the Christians arrived the Druids welcomed them with open arms. The trouble is that the quotation is almost certainly not authentic. There is no trace of it before Merry's book.

Although the Church attempted to wipe out all traces of Druid practice – destroying stone circles, building churches on sites sacred to the Druids – not all was lost. The bardic schools, where poetry, music, story and song were taught, became accepted within the new Christian dispensation, the old stories were written down and the ancient Brehon laws of Ireland, which developed out of the Celtic Druidic culture, were recorded by clerics. Pagan sites continued to attract pilgrimage and worship – the sacred wells of the Celtic goddess Brighid simply became the holy wells of Saint Brighid, for example. And Christians turned other pagan gods and goddesses into saints with extraordinary ease.

CHRISTIANITY BUILDS ON PAGANISM

Christianity seems so substantial and solid, and fundamentalists believe that it is one body of teaching handed to them by God through the Bible. But once you study Christianity, you discover that it has modelled much of its ritual, mythology and structures on the pagan religions from which it evolved. The layout of churches comes from the design of classical pagan temples. The priests' vestments are modelled on classical pagan vestments. Even the church calendar is founded on the pagan festival cycle. The Bible suggests that Jesus was born in the spring or autumn, when shepherds in Judaea watch their flocks. And yet we celebrate his birth at Christmas. Up until the fourth century Jesus' birth was celebrated in May or September. Then it became the custom in Rome to celebrate it at the time of the winter solstice instead. And the same thing applies to many of the other Church festivals – Easter occurs around the spring equinox, Candlemas at Imbolc, the festival of Saint John is at the time of the summer solstice and All Hallows at the time of the pagan feast of Samhuinn.

Even the Bible cannot be seen as a single body of teaching. It has been tampered with ever since it was first put together. Different translations offer different interpretations of key doctrines, and various Church councils have removed parts of the Bible they have disagreed with.

Even though it is not found in the Bible, one of the cornerstones of Christianity is the doctrine of the Trinity, introduced by the Gaulish Bishop Saint Hilary of Poitiers in the third century. Some scholars suggest that the saint was inspired by the Druids, who still flourished in Hilary's third-century Brittany and who organised their ideas in triads and worshipped Goddesses grouped in threes.

Christian baptism was modelled on the Jewish baptism, and according to Irish texts water was used for blessing by the Druids too, way before Christianity. And the mass – which is so central to Christian worship – was already an established feature of the classical pagan mystery traditions, as a sacred feast of bread and wine. Like their festival days, the design of their temples and vestments, and even their sacred sites and some of their saints, the communion feast as a central feature of Christian ritual is not original or unique to Christianity, but existed in paganism long before the arrival of the first Christians.

THE VIRGIN BIRTH AND RESURRECTION

Accounts of the virgin birth and resurrection are found in the pre-Christian world. In the Middle East and Mediterranean basin, stories of virgin births, resurrections and sacrificed saviours were surprisingly common. In the myth of Dionysus, for example, his human mother Semele had an 'immaculate conception', being impregnated not by another human but by the father-god Zeus. Dionysus was born among the animals just as Christ was born in a manger, and was then crucified before descending into a world of darkness and then being reborn. A number of the religions of the Near East and the Mediterranean basin spoke of gods who died and were then reborn, Attis, Tammuz, Adonis and Osiris being among the best known.[19]

The author Robert Graves suggests that the early Celtic Bards, knowing the many other stories of sacrificed gods, might have said to their early Church masters: 'To pretend that [Jesus] was the first whom poets have ever celebrated as having performed these wonderful feats is, despite Saint Paul, to show oneself either hypocritical or illiterate.'[20]

All these similarities do not necessarily negate the power or value of Christianity, and it is important to distinguish between the teachings of Jesus and the institutions which have arisen to spread those teachings. Many of these institutions, with all the political and economic agendas that arise when organisations form, have borrowed, plagiarised, creatively incorporated or ruthlessly crushed many of the spiritual traditions and indigenous cultures they have met on their

way. They have, sadly, been responsible for huge amounts of suffering
– from the tortures of the Inquisition and the burning of heretics and
witches to the bloodshed of the Crusades and countless religious wars.
Nevertheless, none of these facts denies the comfort and guidance
that so many people have gained from Jesus' message.

The power of that message, combined with the Church's intol-
erance of paganism and its determination to succeed without
competition, meant that from the sixth century onwards most
people in Europe had become Christian, even though in remote
rural areas this may have been no more than a nominal Christianity.
Old habits die hard and even in the eleventh century the Church
was still having to rail against 'that most filthy habit' of dressing up
as stags.[21]

AS OPEN PRACTICE DIES OUT, THE INSPIRATION LIVES ON

Despite the tenacity of similar customs throughout the British Isles
and Ireland, and although the indigenous spirituality of Druidism
had flourished openly for around a thousand years, it now had to
survive another millennium in less obvious ways. The Bards were
safely established as minstrels, poets and scribes under the new religion, and the Ovates, who were skilled in healing and prophecy,
must have continued to practise their arts, though with more discre-
tion and with a Christian gloss to their prayers. The Druids, once
Christianity had triumphed over paganism either worked alone or
converted to Christianity. Either way, they remained part of the
professional élite – the scholars, lawyers, teachers and judges – and
although the open practice of Druidism as a religion was extin-
guished, its ideas and inspiration lived on in the cultural and spiritual inheritance of successive generations, encoded in the old tales,
in folklore and in the landscape itself.

By the sixteenth century, however, Druidism had travelled
across the bridge of a thousand years and was about to be reborn in
the Western world.

EXERCISE

Each of us carries a physical, genetic inheritance, and Druids believe we also carry a non-physical, spiritual inheritance which includes the combined experience of our previous lives. In the same way, a spiritual current such as Druidry has both physical transmissions of tradition and spiritual ones. If all books on Druidry and all its current practitioners were to be destroyed, it would still survive to appear again in some form at some time and in some place. Such things are hard for materialist historians to understand. Some psychologists and physicists might find it easier, with their knowledge of the workings of the collective unconscious and of such phenomena as 'morphic resonance'. Things are never what they appear to be and communication can occur in non-physical ways.

This understanding helps us to see that the Druid tradition did not die even when suppressed with the coming of Christianity, but has remained alive and has been transmitted through the centuries because Druidry, Druids and Druid practice are not simply physical. One of the most striking proofs of this lies in the experiences of isolated individuals who meet Druid teachers in their meditations or dreams. These teachers sometimes convey inspiration and practices which accord precisely with traditional Druid practice, even though the individuals concerned knew nothing of Druidry beforehand. In this way, the tree of Druidry grows from within – nourished from a supra-physical source.

After reading this, spend a few moments forgetting all that you have read. Make yourself comfortable and allow yourself to come to a sense of inner centredness and calm. Close your eyes and feel all concerns fall away from you. Focus for a while on your breathing, and then slowly imagine that you are seated on the ground close to an ancient sacred site of the Druids. Touch the earth, smell the air and just let the land and this special place speak to you. You may get specific ideas or thoughts, or you may simply feel or see images. There is a saying in Druidry, 'the Ancients wrote it in the earth'. Imagine you can read this 'writing' – hear it in the wind, feel it in the land.

Listen to its messages, then, when you are ready, become aware of being fully yourself again. Feel full of vitality and strength. Become conscious of your physical body and surroundings, and when you feel ready, open your eyes. Do not stand up quickly – stretch a little before standing up or continuing with the next chapter.

CHAPTER THREE

RENAISSANCE:
THE REBIRTH OF DRUIDRY
IN MODERN TIMES

*The Gods have returned to Eri and have centred themselves in
the sacred mountains and blow the fires through the country.
They have been seen by several in vision. They will awaken the
magical instinct everywhere and the universal heart of
the people will turn to the old Druidic beliefs.*
George Russell ('AE'), in a letter to W. B. Yeats, 1896

The rebirth of Druidry in the modern world can be traced to the
time of the Renaissance, when the forgotten classical texts of
Tacitus, Julius Caesar, Diogenes Laertius and others dealing with the
Druids were rediscovered and eventually printed. By the sixteenth
century virtually all of these texts were available to scholars.

As the British, French and Germans became intrigued by their
pre-Christian ancestry, the discovery of America revealed native
people who seemed to be living in a way similar to that of their own
ancestors, as described by these classical authors. Opinions about

the nature of the Native Americans were divided: some saw them as bloodthirsty and living in 'continuall feare, and danger of violent death . . . [a life] solitary, poore, nasty, brutish and shorte'.[22] Others found that they 'seem to live in that golden worlde of whiche the old writers speake so much . . . the golden worlde without toyle'. In 1584 Arthur Barlowe found the Virginian Indians 'most gentle, loving and faithfull, void of all guile, and treason, and such as lived after the manner of the golden age'. A related opposition of views prevailed with regard to Druidry. Some saw the Druids as evil and primitive human sacrificers, while others saw them as peace-making sages and philosophers – presiding over a body of teachings as dignified as that of the Greeks or the Brahmins.

This polarisation of views continues to this day. Ask a friend what comes to mind when they think of Druids and some will tell you that they think of wise men, guardians of inner wisdom, while others will tell you that they think of virgins being sacrificed by Druids on the 'slaughter stone' of Stonehenge. These divergent views owe their origin to the reports of the classical authors themselves, who conveyed both images to our present-day minds.

Despite this, in Germany and France the availability of the classical texts resulted in a vision of their pre-Roman past that was noble rather than savage. The deep-seated urge to honour one's origins manifested itself in a patriotic pride in these countries, and from 1514 onwards, a series of eulogistic accounts of both Gaulish and German Druids appeared on the Continent.

JOHN AUBREY

In Britain, it was another century before Druids became topics of popular interest. They appeared on stage for the first time in Fletcher's *Bonduca* of 1618 and mention was made of Druids in works such as Drayton's *Polyolbion* of 1622 and Milton's *Lycidas* of 1637. Then, in the 1690s, the Druid Revival began in earnest when John Aubrey, the writer and antiquarian, turned his attention to the stone monuments of Wiltshire.

Aubrey, having studied the classical references to Druidry, carried out pioneering fieldwork at the great monuments of Avebury and Stonehenge. Many of his contemporaries regarded them as of Roman or of later date, but Aubrey realised they were far more ancient and that they were ceremonial centres. He concluded that they were probably used by the Druids. He began work on a book, originally entitled *Templa Druidum* but later changed as its scope widened to *Monumenta Britannica*. Although only excerpts were ever published, the effect of his work was to forge an association between Stonehenge and the Druids which lives in the minds of most people to this day. In Chapter 2 we saw how the latest research makes this association perfectly legitimate. But as recently as the mid 1960s many academics deemed it spurious, prompting Stuart Piggott to write in *The Druids*: 'In Aubrey's tentative association of Stonehenge and other prehistoric stone circles with the Druids was the germ of an idea which was to run like lunatic wildfire through all popular and much learned thought, and particularly emotive feeling, until modern times.'

In many ways John Aubrey can be seen as the real founder of the modern Druid movement. He was inspired by the magical landscape around him, and we can feel proud that a figure of such wit and wisdom presided over Druidry's renaissance.

WILLIAM STUKELEY – FOUNDING FATHER OF ARCHAEOLOGY

John Aubrey's ideas on stone circles influenced another man – William Stukeley. Born in 1687, Stukeley, a young Lincolnshire doctor, had found himself drawn to Stonehenge after seeing engravings of the site. He then read and made notes from a transcript of Aubrey's *Monumenta Britannica*, and a few years later, in 1719, he visited Stonehenge for the first time. For the next five years he made annual visits to Wiltshire, carrying out a detailed study of both Avebury and Stonehenge which laid the foundations for the development of the modern science of archaeology. In 1740 he published the result of his researches in *Stonehenge Restored to the British Druids*.

Stukeley became a Freemason, and discovered – on being summoned to Kew Palace – that the then Princess of Wales shared his enthusiasm for Druidry. She apparently became the patroness of a Druid group that he organised, taking on the name 'Veleda, Archdruidess of Kew'.[23]

THE ANCIENT DRUID ORDER

The Ancient Druid Order, out of which the Order of Bards, Ovates and Druids developed, traces its lineage back to Stukeley, and the philosopher John Toland before him. It is said that Stukeley was succeeded as Chief of the Order by such figures as David Samwell, a medical naval officer who travelled with Captain Cook on *Resolution* and *Discovery*, and who wrote the first-hand account of Cook's death at the hands of natives in Hawaii; William Blake, whose remarkable drawings of Avebury and Stonehenge were strongly influenced by Stukeley and who refused to take the oath at his trial at Chichester Assizes, declaring that he was a Druid; Godfrey Higgins, author of three hefty volumes, the first of which was entitled *Celtic Druids*; Gerald Massey, who was similarly productive, and who – along with Higgins – was used as source material by Mme Blavatsky; and George Watson MacGregor Reid, a flamboyant writer and naturopath who stood for election to both the House of Commons and the American Senate. Historical records can trace leadership of the Ancient Order only to the 1900s, although further research may enable us to trace it further back. It is likely, however, that the earlier figures inspired not so much an actual organisation as a cultural movement and a general interest in Druidry, which resulted at the dawn of the twentieth century in the formation of the Ancient Druid Order (not to be confused with the Ancient Order of Druids, which was founded in 1781, see below).

WELSH DRUIDRY

While these figures guided or inspired English Druidry, Welsh Druidry was strongly influenced by the Glamorganshire stonemason Edward Williams, who took the bardic name Iolo Morganwg. In the late eighteenth century, Morganwg created items of Welsh bardic tradition, based partly or apparently on records, both oral and written, which have since disappeared. Contemporary religious preoccupations combined with his own creative imagination and whatever ancient wisdom records he had inherited to produce a series of literary forgeries which for many years were considered genuine, and resulted in the inclusion of Iolo's now questionable Gorsedd ceremony in the perfectly genuine Eisteddfod. Whether we consider Iolo's influence an inspiration or a pollution, we know that he contributed towards a revival of the bardic tradition in Wales that lives to this day.

THE THREE TYPES OF MODERN DRUIDRY

While the Druid Revival began in the seventeenth century, with interest in the megalithic monuments of Britain and the rediscovered classical texts, it gained momentum in the eighteenth and nineteenth centuries, and resulted in the development of three separate, though related, manifestations of Druidism.

In Wales, Bardic festivals of music and poetry – Eisteddfodau – can be traced back to at least 1176, though they are undoubtedly of ancient provenance. Historical records are scant, however, and the first modern Eisteddfod occurred in 1789. A few years later, in 1792, Iolo Morganwg introduced his Druid ritual into the Eisteddfod proceedings. Since then the Welsh Eisteddfod has grown into a flourishing institution dedicated to helping promote Welsh cultural identity and language, and is now known as the Royal National Eisteddfod of Wales. Most of those who participate in the Eisteddfod

Druid ceremonies would probably be horrified to think their activities might in any way be seen as 'esoteric' or 'pagan'. Much of their spirituality would be grounded in the Church, mostly Methodist, and they would see their Druidic activities as cultural rather than 'spiritual'. The Eisteddfod, complete with its Druid ceremonial, was also adopted in Brittany in 1899 and in Cornwall in 1928.[24]

In England a different kind of Druidism developed through the organisation of the Ancient Order of Druids, founded by Henry Hurle in a tavern in London's Poland Street in 1781. Modelled along the lines of Freemasonry, it offered mutual support, social gatherings, and a type of ceremonial similar to those of fraternal societies, where a Bible was placed on the lectern at each meeting and discussion of religion was prohibited. Lodges proliferated throughout England, and then abroad in most corners of the British Empire and in parts of Europe. Schisms occurred and other groups formed, and many thousands of people were (and still are) members of such groups. As with Freemasonry, engraved certificates, rings and even porcelain tea sets are sometimes discovered in antique shops or are unearthed as ancestral heirlooms, and families remember that 'Granddad was a Druid'. But even though the Druid was offered as a symbol of the wise philosopher within such groups, no spiritual teachings were given, and their purpose was seen as exclusively charitable and social.

The third type of Druidry that evolved as a result of the revival of interest in Druidism was practised in England by the Ancient Druid Order. Only here do we see an attempt to make Druidry a spiritual path in its own right. Early in the 1900s, if not before, the Order began holding summer solstice rites at Stonehenge – initiating a struggle with the owners of the land to gain access for worship that has continued on and off for about a hundred years. In addition, autumn and spring equinox ceremonies started to be held annually on Primrose Hill and Tower Hill in London. Initiation ceremonies were developed and esoteric teachings given.

THE WIDER WORLD –
BEYOND THE ORGANISED DRUIDS

So far we have looked at how organised Druidry has evolved over the last few centuries. But in many ways the real resurgence of Druidry occurred outside the limited circles of the Welsh, Cornish and Breton Eisteddfod movements, the English fraternal societies and – later – London's occult intelligentsia.

Ever since the rediscovery of the old classical texts and the simultaneous discovery of the New World, the Druids had come to symbolise a hidden history. The prevailing view that our pre-Christian ancestors had been ignorant, grunting savages was undermined by the image of robed 'forest sages' who taught Pythagorean mathematics to the children of the nobility, and who parted warring factions with soothing words of wisdom, 'shaming Mars before the Muses' as Diodorus Siculus recounted. The Romantics loved this, and the Druids came to represent an indigenous lineage of noble philosophers that had previously been thought to exist only on foreign soil – in the classical worlds of Greece and Rome.

This new-found pride in ancestry coincided with the movement away from imperialism and towards nationalism. Local pride in local culture, folklore and language developed, so that customs and folk-tales that had been dismissed as quaint or irrelevant now began to feed the newly developing national literatures of Ireland, Wales and Scotland. And in the background stood the Druid – half shrouded in the mists of fantasy and wish-fulfilment, half-revealed in the light of lingering custom or ancient tale.

This revival of interest and the gaining of inspiration from Celtic mythology – from stories and accounts of the old Gods and the ancient Druids – has never diminished. The Romantic poets and philosophers found their inspiration there, as did the writers and poets of the Celtic Twilight. Celtic art and music has continued to haunt our imaginations and to feed our souls. Slowly, over the last three hundred years since the beginnings of the Druid Revival, the treasure-chest of our western European pre-Christian spiritual heritage has been revealed, and the effect of this has only really become apparent in the last few decades, with Druidry and Celtic spirituality gaining their rightful places, finally, alongside the other great spiritual traditions of the world.

EXERCISE

After reading this chapter, spend a few moments forgetting all that you have read, make yourself comfortable and allow yourself to come to a sense of inner centredness and calm. Let all disturbing thoughts be laid aside. Close your eyes, and focus for a few moments on your breathing. Become aware of the sun rising. Feel yourself bathed in light and warmth. Become this light and warmth if it feels right. Now open your eyes and read this passage, allowing your creative imagination to build the images as you learn of them:

Imagine that you are living in Britain in the seventeenth century. A friend hands you copies of the classical authors' writings on Druidry. That evening, by candlelight, you read Caesar, Strabo, Diodorus Siculus and others, who tell of the Druids and of their meetings in groves. That night you dream that you have travelled back in time and are consulting with a Druid in a sacred grove. You are given helpful and inspiring guidance.

The following day you remember that near where you live is a stone circle – perhaps Avebury or Stonehenge. You pack food and drink, mount your horse and ride there with a companion. You find local farmers trying to break up the stones. You talk with them, persuading them that the circle represents a part of their heritage. They leave. You walk among the stones, touching them and admiring their simple power and beauty.

Evening falls, and as the stars begin to shine above you, you spend the warm summer night sitting among the stones. With your companion you resolve to form a society to research the meaning of these sacred places, and you decide to make a journey soon to the Bards of Wales to see if you might learn more of the Druids and their lore.

For a moment you fall asleep, and in your sleep a Druid comes to you to say: 'We are always here. Watching and waiting. We will guide and counsel and protect you. The ancient wisdom was known to us in the past and it can be known again. The stars speak through the stones. Light shines in the densest matter. Earth and heaven are one. Our physical beings and our heavenly souls are united in the mystery of being.'

You wake up among the stones. You return home with your companion on horseback. You see yourself looking in the candle-light at the manuscripts given to you by your friend. You become aware of looking at this book now. You feel yourself fully present in your physical body – here and now – filled with vitality and health.

CHAPTER FIVE

DRUIDISM TODAY:

A MODERN MYSTERY SCHOOL

*Every spiritual tradition has a complex history, and the histories of
minority movements such as modern paganism are more complex than
most. Rather than defining Druidry in mythic terms as a primal tradition
of the distant past – to be investigated purely by means of historical
research, and thus distanced from the present – it makes more sense to
treat it in historical terms as an evolving system changing constantly
through time, subject to periodic interruptions, renewals, reformula-
tions, outside influences, and the impact of individual experiences.*

John Michael Greer, *Awen – A Book of Druid Lore*

We have seen how the Druids emerge out of the mists of
prehistory as possibly the proto-Druidic builders of stone
circles, until they enter written history as the Druids of the classical
authors, flourishing for as long perhaps as a thousand years, until in

the sixth century they seem to disappear as Christianity becomes the sole religion. For another thousand years the ideas and practices of Druidry become enshrined in popular culture through the recording of the old tales by Christian clerics, and through Christianity's adoption of pagan customs, until – through the sixteenth, seventeenth and eighteenth centuries – a revival of interest in Druidry occurs which results in the founding of Druid groups. Some of these groups are simply inspired by the idea of Druids, while in reality they are cultural or fraternal organisations, with almost exclusively male and Christian memberships. But other groups are interested in Druidry as a spiritual path – they see Druidism as one of the ancient mystery traditions, and want the mystery school of the Druids to open its doors once again to seekers in the modern world.

THE ANCIENT DRUID ORDER AND THE ORDER OF BARDS, OVATES AND DRUIDS

One such group was the Ancient Druid Order, which my teacher, Ross Nichols, joined in 1954. He became Maenarch (Chairman) of the Order until, with colleagues, he formed the Order of Bards, Ovates and Druids a decade later. The teachings and ceremonies of the Ancient Druid Order, while inspired by the classical accounts of the Druids, drew mostly on the material of Iolo Morganwg, combined with influences from the magical Order of the Golden Dawn and the Theosophists, rather than on the inspiration of Celtic mythology and folklore, and when Ross finally left the Order he was able to re-introduce a focus on this core material. The teachings of the new group that he formed were organised into the three traditional grades of learning recorded by the classical authors, of Bard, Ovate and Druid. A study of Celtic mythology, the bardic craft of poetry and the Ogham tree-language was introduced, and the full round of eight seasonal ceremonies were celebrated, as opposed to the three celebrated by the Ancient Order.

It had taken a long time – from the Druid Revival several

hundred years previously – for Druidry to reclaim its essential focus and its source material. The preoccupation of eighteenth-century revivalists with seeing Druidry as a precursor to Christianity, and of nineteenth-century Theosophists and Universalists with seeing it as yet another manifestation of the Perennial Philosophy, had obscured the unique and dynamic qualities that Druidry offered the modern world. It was these qualities that Ross perceived and which he introduced into modern Druid practice, thereby making him a seminal figure in the story of Druidism.

Ross introduced into the world what one scholar now calls 'Traditional British Druidry'[25] at a time of massive cultural ferment – the 1960s. Gerald Gardner, with the help of Ross, had introduced 'Traditional British Wicca' to the public a decade previously. Both men drew on folklore, mythology and the Western magical tradition to create new kinds of spiritual practice rooted in the pre-Christian traditions of the British Isles and Ireland. While Gardner roamed far and wide in his search for the ingredients for his Wiccan practice, Ross concentrated on Celtic mythology and on a study of bardism and the old sacred sites for his articulation of Druidism.

The 1960s heralded a surge of interest in new approaches to life and spirituality, and midway through this decade, a turning point in Ross's life occurred. In one year – 1964 – three of his friends and mentors died. They were spiritual leaders in the fields of Druidry, Wicca and Christianity: Robert MacGregor Reid, the Chief of the Ancient Druid Order, Gerald Gardner and Archbishop Tugdual, who had ordained Ross in the Ancient Celtic Church the year previously. It was time for Ross to become a leader himself.

NUINN – THE OLD CHIEF DRUID

This was about the time I first met Ross – as he and a group of fellow Druids formed the Order of Bards, Ovates and Druids after the death of the old Chief of the Ancient Order. I and a friend, both of us twelve years old, interviewed him about Stonehenge and Druidry for a magazine we had started. My memories of this meeting are vague, but I remember feeling at ease with this man who rummaged through his papers to show us charts and diagrams of the old monuments.

Four years later I met Ross again, at a time when I was fascinated by photography. He too was a keen photographer, and during our conversation he invited me to photograph the ceremonies. Every six weeks or so I would travel to Parliament Hill in Highgate or to the Alliance Hall in Victoria, and found myself increasingly wanting to participate in rather than photograph these ceremonies.

When I visited Ross, or Nuinn as he was known in the Order (Nuinn is Irish for the ash tree), we would begin our meetings by poring over the proofs of the photographs I had taken – often drinking tea and eating sandwiches. But we would soon move on to talking about Druidry and the esoteric. After a few months, photography was dispensed with, and our meetings were concerned solely with spiritual matters. I had been drawn to Buddhism when I was about eleven and by the age of sixteen was keen to know all I could of every kind of esoteric lore. Nuinn, now in his sixties, had spent all his adult life studying religion, mythology and the occult, and being an historian he seemed able to retain the sort of detail which my mind struggled to remember. He was particularly fond of scribbling little notes and diagrams on the backs of envelopes or on napkins when we met in a café near his office in Gloucester Road. He was the principal of a 'crammer' – a college that specialised in cramming information into students who had failed their exams. At Carlisle and Gregson's or 'Jimmy's', as it was called, there was no sport, no assembly, no distraction from the serious business of fact-stuffing and exam taking. It was to Jimmy's that Winston Churchill (also a Druid, though of the fraternal variety) was sent after failing his exams for Sandhurst.

Ross sometimes held grove meetings in an empty classroom or in the staff common room at Jimmy's, when the building had emptied for the evening. He made no secret of his connection with Druidry. His secretary seemed to spend most of her time typing Order correspondence or teaching material. Occasionally a member of staff or student would be intrigued enough to come to one of the public lectures he organised, or to attend one of the public ceremonies.

His work as a college principal had accustomed him to teaching and to coaching individual pupils – and this is really what he did with me. We hardly ever talked personally – each time we met we got straight down to business. And our business was Druidry and a study of the occult. I would arrive at his house several times a week after school and he would just say hello, put the kettle on, and perhaps offer a sandwich left over from lunchtime. Occasionally he would cook something – he once taught me how to make a nut rissole. The kettle would boil, he would make two cups of tea, and we would move from the kitchen to an adjacent room which was used for ceremonies and as an overflow classroom for the college a mile away.

He would then take one of the teaching discourses of the Order and read it out to me. Having done this, he would begin again at the beginning, picking out the important points and expanding on related themes. He might then scribble a diagram to clarify the subject, and conclude by talking about the Order in one way or another. I would then leave, having been mostly silent except to question anything I didn't understand.

What I didn't realise at the time was that this man, who was exactly fifty years older than me, would come to be seen long after his death as one of the two founding figures of modern paganism, alongside his friend Gerald Gardner.

INITIATION

After several years I asked if I could join the Order, and at the age of eighteen was initiated on Glastonbury Tor at Beltane to the accompaniment of music by the Third Ear Band.

Once a fortnight Nuinn held an open meditation group, to which half a dozen or so people would come. Some were members of the Order, some were not. After giving a guided meditation, he would meticulously note down the experience of each member of the group and make remarks when he felt they would be helpful or when he saw connections between the different experiences. He was particularly interested in the way experiences in a group medi-tation are often related to the position in which one sits in a circle, and the way related positions reflect similar experiences. Often he would ask his secretary to type out the notes he made and would distribute them at the next meeting. He would sometimes draw lines between those positions in the circle which seemed to have connections.

Nuinn wasn't a guru and made no effort to be considered as one. His failings and his humanity were as clearly visible as his capacities and talents. He had the breadth of knowledge of a man who had spent his life in academic and esoteric work, free from the constraints of rearing a family. But freedom and independence had left their mark, and there was a certain loneliness about him. He had no television, but instead busied himself with study and research. Occasionally he displayed the sort of crotchety ill-humour that is characteristic of the elderly who live on their own, but on the whole he was accessible and friendly to everyone he met, and one of his warmest characteristics was the way in which he praised, and in my opinion grossly over-estimated, everybody's talents and abilities. Everyone he knew was accomplished at something – either he was immensely naive or he was applying one of the prime tenets of the positive thought movement, and seeing people for what they could be rather than simply for what they were.

In his time he had had a fair number of knocks. He suffered from asthma, his schooldays were unhappy, his brother was killed by friendly fire during the war and Jimmy's always appeared to be going through some crisis or another – of either money or staff or students. In the occult realm he had brushes with several malevolent magi-cians, and we talked at length about these. Despite these difficulties he was able to travel extensively: he visited Egypt and Morocco, Greece and Bulgaria, Malta and France, Ireland and the Outer Hebrides. On each of these visits he made sketches, took photo-graphs, and made endless notes – some of which he turned into witty and scholarly journals.

THE OCCULT ESTABLISHMENT
AND PUBLICATIONS

Ross had met many of the famous figures in the occult establishment of his day – Aleister Crowley and Alex Sanders, J. G. Bennett and Idries Shah among others. But he always kept his own counsel. He enjoyed meeting people, and bringing them together. Nowadays we would call him a 'networker'. He held parties in his house, often before a ceremony such as Imbolc or Samhuinn, which were private, invitation-only celebrations.

Besides leading the Order, Ross managed to pursue a career as a poet. Three books of his poetry were published, and a new selection of his work chosen and introduced by the contemporary poet Jay Ramsay was published in 2001.[26] He also contributed many articles on Druidry, the occult and exoteric history to such journals as *Man Myth and Magic*, *The Ley Hunter* and my father's magazine, *Past and Future*. He was also assistant editor and contributor to *The Occult Observer* in 1949 and 1950.

In 1952 he published a twin-volume edition of Paul Christian's eighteenth-century French work *The History and Practice of Magic*, which he had edited and combined with articles by friends on astrology and palmistry. He also edited his friend Gerald Gardner's book *Witchcraft Today*, which appeared in 1954 and which marked the beginning of the popularisation of Wicca in modern times. In addition, Ross wrote two books of his own: the manuscript of one, *The Land of the White Bull*, has been lost but the second, *The Book of Druidry*, which he completed just before his death, was published posthumously in 1990. And as if this were not enough for one lifetime, Nuinn was also an accomplished water-colourist, with some of his work being exhibited at the Royal Institute gallery in London.

NATURISM AND THE
WOODLAND RETREAT

Ross was a committed naturist, joining the Utopian Spielplatz community in Hertfordshire in the 1930s and later Gerald Gardner's Five Acres club – which he visited regularly until the end of his life. In addition, to create a place of refuge where he could be close to nature and where he could paint and write without the distractions of the city, he bought a piece of woodland in Buckinghamshire. There he installed three huts – one for himself and two for guests – furnished simply with camp beds and cooking pots. There he was able to live in utter simplicity. In the privacy of the woods he was able to feel that contact with nature which comes when we free ourselves of all trappings – both psychic and physical. He was able to gather wood, cook over an open fire and nourish himself with the power of the trees and the stars before returning to his work as Order Chief and college principal, historian, artist and poet.[27]

I have painted this picture of my Druid teacher in some detail because I want to convey the qualities of a modern Druid, and he was a fine example. He was able to combine strong artistic abilities with an enquiring logical mind. He enjoyed working with ceremonial and being in close contact with nature. His viewpoint was eclectic, not limited – he was always studying, to the very end of his life – whether it was the Qabala or Wicca or Sufism. But despite his natural paganism, and his devotion to Druidry, he always remained a Christian and was a regular visitor to his local church. Even so, he struggled to accept Christianity – and one can observe this struggle in two revealing critiques he wrote of Christianity, published in *In the Grove of the Druids – The Druid Teachings of Ross Nichols*. During the sixties, the time of flower power, he tried his best to understand what was happening with the young in Britain. The psychedelic review *The International Times* published a letter of his on William Blake, and he knew and admired the work of John Michell, a leading figure in 1960s counter-culture, who popularised the concepts of ley lines and astro-archaeology with his cult bestseller *A View Over Atlantis*.[28]

FROM THE FRINGE TO THE CENTRE

After the death of Ross in 1975 Druidry gradually moved from the fringes of alternative spirituality to its centre – alongside other spiritual movements that offered a different approach to the established religions. Over the following decades people the world over turned in their thousands to the earth religions and indigenous spiritualities, including Druidry – and steadily a plethora of books, groups and websites on Druidism began to appear. Soon there were many varieties of Druidry, as different groups were inspired to interpret it in different ways. Some groups and books were highly eclectic as they drew on multiple strands of inspiration, which included New Age thought, Wiccan practice and modern approaches to shamanism, while others concentrated their efforts on attempting to reconstruct what they believed to be authentic ancient beliefs and practices.

Despite these differences, however, certain themes were almost universally adopted: the reverence for nature, an avoidance of dogmatism or the development of a priesthood or spiritual hierarchy, and an absence of discrimination on the basis of gender, age, race or sexual orientation. Some people find Druidry frustrating because it seems to be a spirituality that operates with very few beliefs and no particular or universally agreed theology. But others find this liberating. The success of Druidry today is living proof of the fact that we can find spiritual inspiration, support, guidance and community from an approach to life that is free of dogma and theology. How each Druid conceives of Deity is up to them – some are monists or monotheists, believing that there is just one cosmic force that encompasses all creation, others are pantheists, seeing divinity in nature, some duotheists, believing Deity to be God and Goddess, and others are polytheists, believing that there are many gods. Some will believe their god(s) and/or goddess(es) are actual beings, others will sense them as archetypes or metaphors for unfathomable cosmic forces, while others will take an agnostic approach – saying they simply do not know what to think or believe.

One of the most remarkable attributes of contemporary Druidism is that one can find such widely different approaches within it. Despite, or perhaps because of, its refusal to be dogmatic about that which is essentially unknowable it occupies a unique position in contemporary spirituality.

EXERCISE

After reading this chapter, spend a few moments forgetting all that you have read, make yourself comfortable and allow yourself to come to a sense of inner centredness and calm. Let all disturbing thoughts be laid aside. Close your eyes, and focus for a few moments on your breathing. Become aware of the sun rising. Feel yourself bathed in light and warmth. Become this light and warmth if it feels right. Now open your eyes and read this passage, allowing your creative imagination to build the images as you learn of them:

Imagine that a friend invites you to a Druid ceremony. You are intrigued and amused. 'Do Druids still exist?' you ask your friend. He or she suggests you find out by coming along. You experience some anxiety as you travel to the house of a Druid in the country. You feel that you might be about to meet some very odd characters. You are relieved to find a group of people who seem in many ways unremarkable in their ordinariness – their 'everydayness'. After chatting briefly, you leave the house to gather in a small grove in the woods near to the house. Almost imperceptibly the 'everydayness' of the people and the surroundings changes. One by one each person steps into the sacred circle. Now it is your turn. As you step forward, you feel its strength and its power – its sacredness and its protection. The ceremony begins and you find it inspiring, calming, moving.

When it is over, it is your turn to step out of the circle. As you do so, you feel yourself returning to the everyday world. But somehow it is different. You look at your friend, at the others. You realise that they are, and they are not, Druids. You realise it is a label like any other, for we need words to communicate and to define.

Gradually you become aware of holding this book in your hands, and of being fully yourself here and now, before standing up and stretching.

CHAPTER SIX

BARDS, OVATES AND DRUIDS

*Among all the Gallic peoples, generally speaking, there are three
sets of men who are held in exceptional honour: the Bards, the
Vates, and the Druids. The Bards are singers and poets; the
Vates, diviners and natural philosophers; while the Druids, in
addition to natural philosophy, study also moral philosophy.*

Strabo, *Geographica*, written at the end of the first century BC

Now that we have briefly surveyed the history of Druidry from
ancient times to the present, it is time to explore the three
types of Druid that were said to exist – and to see whether they have
any relevance for us today.

The classical writers tell us that the ancient Druids organised
themselves into three distinct groupings, and each group had
specific functions and tasks to perform, and a specific training.

BARDS

*And there are among them composers of verses whom they
call Bards; these singing to instruments similar to a lyre,
applaud some, while they vituperate others.*

(Diodorus Siculus, *Histories*, 8 BC)

The Bards were the keepers of tradition, of the memory of the tribe –
they were the custodians of the sacredness of the Word. Although they
probably represented the first level of training for an apprentice Druid,
we should not make the mistake of thinking that a Bard was somehow
in a lowly or inferior position. There were many levels of accomplishment, but the most skilled of Bards were held in high esteem and
partook of many of the functions of both the Ovate and the Druid.

The training of a Bard was intense and lasted for many years.
There were variations in the curricula between Scotland, Ireland
and Wales. In Ireland it is recorded that the training lasted twelve
years, with students undergoing the following rigorous curriculum:
In the first year, the student progressed from Principle Beginner
(Ollaire) to Poet's Attendant (Tamhan) to Apprentice Satirist
(Drisac). During this time they had to learn the basics of the bardic
arts: grammar, twenty stories and the Ogham tree-alphabet.

Over the next four years, they learned a further ten stories each
year, a hundred Ogham combinations, a dozen philosophy lessons,
and an unspecified number of poems. They also studied diphthongal
combinations, the Law of Privileges and the uses of grammar.

By the sixth year any student who had stayed the course was
called a Pillar (Cli) and would study a further forty-eight poems and
twenty more stories. Over the following three years, the Pillars were
termed Noble Streams (Anruth) because 'a stream of pleasing praise
issues from him, and a stream of wealth to him'. During this time
they learned a further ninety-five tales, bringing their repertoire up
to 175. They studied prosody, glosses, prophetic invocation, the
styles of poetic composition, specific poetic forms and the place-
name stories of Ireland.

The final three years of training brought elevation to Ollamh, or Doctor of Poetry. In the tenth year the student had to study further poetic forms and composition, in the eleventh year 100 poems and in the twelfth year 120 orations and the four arts of poetry. The student was now the master or mistress of 350 stories in all.

As Anruth, students had carried a silver branch, and before that – since the beginning of their training – they had carried a bronze branch. An Ollamh was entitled to receive a gold branch. All these branches had bells attached to them, so that any poet striding into the hall to recite a poem or tell a tale would be accompanied by the sound of bells – warning the audience to become silent and summoning the help of the inner realms to ensoul the forthcoming poem or story.

In Wales and Scotland the training of a Bard was similarly rigorous, although with different grades and a different curriculum.

HOW WERE THE BARDS TRAINED?

Bardic schools formed around a Chief Poet and their attendants. A good deal of time was spent in learning by rote, to strengthen the memory and learn the fantastic number of tales and poems required of an accomplished Bard.

Records from both the Western Highlands and Ireland show that much work was undertaken through the technique we would now term sensory deprivation. The accommodation was Spartan in the extreme, and much time would be spent incubating poems and seeking inspiration in total darkness. It is only comparatively recently that we have rediscovered, through the pioneering work of John Lilly, the fertile power of the darkness found in an isolation tank.[29]

The curriculum shows that the students were accumulating in memory a vast store of stories and poems. But this was only half their work. They were training to become masters of both record *and* inspiration. It was only one of their duties to record the lore, laws and genealogy of the tribe. Just as important as this task of keeping alive tradition and heritage, they were entrusted with knowledge of the sacred power of the Word – manifest as the ability to become inspired and to inspire others. To carry the records of the tribe they needed to know the stories and poems which preserved the lineage and the lore of their people, but to be Masters or Mistresses of Inspiration they needed to compose their own poems and tales. It was for this reason that they underwent sensory deprivation and employed the arts of invocation. Such training naturally awoke inner powers. A powerful memory, and an ability to plumb the depths and roam the heights of consciousness in search of inspiration and the creative flame, developed within the Bard an ability to see into the future and influence the world around them in a way that foreshadowed the work of the Ovate and the Druid, and which allowed them to carry the spirit of Druidry through the centuries when the light of both the Ovate and the Druid could not be seen in the world.

It is fitting that this first level or grade of Druid training should so encompass both the Ovate and the Druid work. It seems that the Druid would concur with the opening words of John's gospel: 'In the beginning was the Word'. The way in which the Word could create, command, nourish, heal, cut through, purify, invoke, unite, provoke, deter and bind was a power that the Bard through long training came to know and utilise in the service of their patron, their king or queen, their Druid, and their god or goddess.

> O Hear the voice of the Bard
> Who present, past and future sees
> Whose ears have heard the holy Word
> That walked among the ancient trees . . .
> (William Blake, first 'Song of Experience')

Now that we know something of what the Bards did and how they were trained, we can ask ourselves what relevance Bardic work might have for us today.

In the training of the Order of Bards, Ovates and Druids, we begin our study in Druidry with the bardic grade – and this is deeply meaningful. Bardism is understood in its widest sense as the development of the artistic and creative self, and its importance as a foundation for our lives and character and spiritual development is no less significant than it was thousands of years ago. Indeed, it could be argued that it is even more essential today than it was then. The clue to understanding why this should be so lies in the realisation that the historical Bards worked with record and with inspiration. One of the prime reasons for modern humanity's sense of alienation lies in the fact that we have cut ourselves adrift from both the natural world and from the roots of our past. Practising Druidry is about healing this alienation – reconnecting to our past and to the world of nature. In the bardic grade we open ourselves to the inspiration of the natural world, and we allow the mandala of the eightfold seasonal cycle, explained in the next chapter, to be grounded in our beings. Working with record means working with heritage, lineage, and the mythology and stories of the tribe – it helps us reconnect to the past.

Working with inspiration means opening ourselves to our innate creativity. Many of the problems that we suffer from in the developed world result from our suppression and denial of the artistic – in all its forms. Modern brain research shows that for most of us, our primary mode of functioning comes from the dominant cerebral hemisphere, which mediates the function of analytical thinking. The opposite hemisphere has less of a say in our current way of living – it is the hemisphere that mediates the synthesising, non-analytic forms of thought and expression: it is the part of the brain considered responsible for artistic expression. It is generally agreed that to become complete we need to allow both sides of ourselves adequate opportunities for development and expression. This truth was expressed by the alchemists (and there is a strong tradition of alchemy within Druidry) and later by Carl Jung (whose work first began to influence modern Druidry through Ross Nichols). Jung developed his theory of the personal *animus* and *anima* – male and female aspects of the psyche – which for our development need to relate and periodically conjoin. Alchemists knew of the importance of this conjunction, and they termed it the mystical marriage or the *mysterium coniunctionis*.

Our education has, for the most part, concentrated on developing our skills of analytical and mathematical thinking, but when we enter the bardic way, we begin a process that develops our less dominant hemisphere. We open ourselves to the artistic, the creative self. This is no simple task, and in a way typical of Druidry, the work is undertaken in an apparently roundabout fashion. Through working with the eightfold festival scheme, and with the power of the four elements that are allocated to the cardinal points in the sacred circle of Druid working, the Bard is brought to a stage where they have acknowledged and worked with the four aspects of their being – represented by earth, their practicality and sensuality; water, their receptivity and feelings; air, their reasoning; and fire, their intuition and enthusiasm. As these four elements and parts of the self are explored and harmonised, the Bard finds him- or herself naturally opening to their inner creativity. Gradually the resources of body and heart, mind and intuition become more fully available to guide and inspire them.

By working in this way we learn to by-pass the rational mind, which so loves to create limits to understanding. To be able to operate, the intellect creates distinctions, categories, mental constructions – through which experience can be comprehended and acted upon. This is essential for our survival and progress in the world. The problems arise when this ability to create frames of reference is not counter-balanced by the ability to transcend these frames and open oneself to the transrational – the inexplicable in words but no less true. Poetry and music are supremely competent at helping us to go beyond frames and viewpoints. Sound – spoken, sung or played – stretches our boundaries, opens horizons, invokes energies that the intellect alone cannot grasp or categorise with its workings. Here is the power of the Bard – to dissolve our boundaries, our frames of reference – even if only for a moment.

Take this poem, by the modern Bard Jay Ramsay:

> Fathomless unknown,
> Behind and in everything –
> Valley – kestrel – celandine:
> You nowhere, and in everything –

And being nothing, being silenced,
Being unable to speak
You see everything,
And I see You
And I see I am
The core I am seeing:

The sun closening
To meet the man
Who has crossed the line,
Who has walked out of himself

Stands ahead there,
Naked in the light.

One's mind cannot fully grasp the power of such a poem – one is struck by the force of the words and imagery in a way that defies description or explanation. This is the work of poetry – of the Bard. To go beyond. To travel. To bring back.

Professor Michael Harner, a world authority on shamanism, speaks of the shamanic way as one which is best defined as a method to open a door and enter a different reality.[30] This is precisely what happens with powerful and effective poetry. The difference between 'secular' poetry writing, reading and reciting and the same activities undertaken in the spirit of bardism is that in the latter this shamanic process is consciously acknowledged and worked with. Creativity and inspiration are seen as gifts of the gods, as powers entering the vessel of the self through the superconscious. Appropriate preparation, ritual, visualisation, prayer and meditation create the channels through which such generative, creative power can flow. In Druidry this power is known as 'awen', which is Welsh for 'inspiration' or 'flowing spirit'.

The relevance of this work to the contemporary artistic scene is clear: when art became secularised, what it gained in freedom of expression it lost in depth of inspiration. Now we have turned full circle and are able to spiritualise our art once again – freed at last from the limitations of religious dogma. The potential for enhanced creativity is immense when we recontextualise our creativity in terms of the sacred. Previously this involved being bound by Christian themes and dogma. Now it means recognising the sacredness not only of the spirit, but of the earth and the four elements, and of our body and sexuality too.

The Bardic stream is not simply a body of knowledge we once possessed and which we attempt to regain – it is a spiritualised mode of artistic creative consciousness which is dynamic and living – the future holds as much promise, if not more, than the past.

In addition to reciting poetry and story-telling, the Bards undoubtedly made music and danced. There are intriguing stories of Druid dances remembered in Brittany, and it is possible that traces of this early sacred and celebratory dancing is contained within morris dancing, the Abbot's Bromley horn dance and other folk dances. Our challenge is to rediscover the music, chants and dances of the Druids – by contacting the archetypal sources of inspiration within. These sources are transpersonal and out-of-time. They fed the Druids in the past and they can feed us now. We know some of the instruments they probably would have used: in the early days of animistic proto-Druidry they would most likely have used flutes made from birds' bones (eagle-bone flutes have been found in Scotland). They would probably have banged stones on hollow ringing rocks to produce a bell-like sound. The dord, a form of horn with a sound like the Australian Aborigine's didgeridoo, was clearly a sacred instrument of the Bronze Age, as were almost certainly an animal-skin drum which later evolved into the bodhran, and the claves – two sticks of wood which were banged together to produce a rhythm alone or counterpoised with that of the drum.[31]

Those who choose to explore Druidry by entering the bardic course of the Order of Bards, Ovates and Druids open themselves to what it means to be living on the earth with the ability to be creative. Although this is the first stage of Druid training, its purpose reaches to the very heart of Druidry – which is the development of an intimate knowledge of the powers of generation – at the bardic level this involves the generation of creative works – of music, song, poetry and art in all its forms.

In common with oral indigenous spiritual traditions the world over, the ancient Druids encoded their teachings in story form. The Bards learned these stories and were therefore able to preserve the memory of the teachings across the centuries, despite the fact that they were never written down. Fortunately for us, the Christian scribes recorded these tales, and even though some details may have been omitted or distorted, we can still discern the teachings of the Druids encoded within them. One such story is the Tale of Taliesin, which recounts the progress of a young boy who eventually becomes the finest Bard in the land. He does this by drinking three drops of awen – inspiration – from the cauldron of the goddess Ceridwen.

In the distance-learning programme of the Order, as we enter the bardic grade we are told this story and then are invited to explore it in depth over a year, since encoded within the tale is an entire curriculum that shows each of us how we can become the 'finest Bard'. The story of the young person's journey towards a full flowering of creativity interacts with our own personal story, gradually helping to release the Bard, the creative self, within.

The tree which represents the bardic grade is the birch – appropriately it is the first tree of the Druid's Ogham tree-alphabet, and the tree which represents new beginnings, pioneering and giving birth. The west is the place of the Bard. It is from the west that we enter the circle in Druid ceremonies, and the west is therefore the place of entrance, of beginnings – the receptive, feminine west that faces the east of the dawn ray. The times associated with the bardic grade are the spring and dawn – times when we are fresh and ready to begin a new cycle of learning and experience.

OVATES

To you alone it is given to know the truth about the gods and deities of the sky . . . The innermost groves of far-off forests are your abodes. And it is you who say that the shades of the dead seek not

the silent land of Erebus and the pale halls of Pluto; rather, you tell
us that the same spirit has a body again elsewhere, and that death,
if what you sing is true, is but the mid-point of long life.

(Lucan, *Pharsalia, circa* AD 60)

Lucan, in the above quotation, is addressing Druids generally, but it
is an appropriate quotation to open our study of the Ovates, for it
was they who, to the greatest degree, were responsible for understanding the mysteries of death and rebirth, for transcending time –
for divining the future, for conversing with the ancestors – travelling beyond the grave to bring augury and counsel to those still
living on earth.

If the Bards were shamans in Michael Harner's understanding
of the term because they opened doors with the power of the Word,
then the Ovates deserve the term shaman even more so – for they
open the doors of time.

From a study of the classical authors, a general categorisation of
the three different grades accords the arts to the Bards, the skills of
prophecy and divination to the Ovates and philosophical, teaching,
counselling and judicial tasks to the Druid.

The Ovates, then, were seers and diviners, travellers in time,
and it seems likely that they were also healers, herbalists and
midwives. The English word 'Ovate' comes from the various terms
used by the classical writers: *Vates, Uatis, Euhages,* which may derive
from the Indo-European root *uat,* 'to be inspired or possessed'. The
classical author Strabo described the Ovate as 'an interpreter of
nature'. It was the Ovates who were skilled in reading omens and
divining auguries – whether from the flight of birds, the shape of
clouds, or the behaviour of animals or the weather – and it was the
Ovates whose task it probably was to heal, using their knowledge of
herbs and spells to cure disease in humans and livestock. The Ovate
seems, in many ways, to conform to the type of person most people
would describe as a witch, and it is certainly possible that when
Druidry went underground with the coming of Christianity, the
Ovate stream may have become a source that fed later generations
of healers and followers of the Old Ways, until they came to be

known as the Cunning Folk – healers who could still be found in villages in Britain up until the 1930s. And it is quite possible that these cunning people were in fact the witches of modern popular perception.

The Ovate as master or mistress of prophecy and divination needed, and still needs today, a reorientation in relation to time. To travel within time – to read the Akashic records as some would term it – requires a conception of its nature and dynamics that is radically different from post-Enlightenment thinking, and more akin to the understanding now being offered by the New Physics.

The belief in the cyclicity of life, as we shall see in the next chapter, was fundamental to the worldview of the ancient Druids. In common with Eastern religions, the Druids believed in reincarnation. Caesar, in *De Bello Gallico*, says of the Druids: 'The cardinal doctrine which they seek to teach is that souls do not die, but after death pass from one to another; and this belief, as the fear of death is thereby cast aside, they hold to be the greatest invective to valour.' Diodorus quotes Posidonius when he says that the Druids held that 'the souls of men are immortal, and that after a definite number of years they live a second life when the soul passes to another body'. And Philostratus of Tyana in the second century noted that the Celts believed that to be born in this world, we have to die in the Otherworld, and conversely, that when we die here, our birth into the Otherworld should be celebrated.[32]

Now we can understand how the Ovates were able to conceive of time-travel. The realm of the ancestors was not the realm of people dead-and-gone – it was the repository of tribal wisdom – the realm in which the ancestors lived whilst awaiting reincarnation and to which the Ovate could turn for guidance and inspiration on behalf of the tribe. The experience of the shaman is one in which they undergo some type of death but return to life – only this time knowing the inner soul-geography. In the past, this experience of returning to life from the realm of death was a rare occurrence. With today's sophisticated resuscitation techniques, the experience is becoming more frequent. A growing academic interest in the subject means that we now have an enormous amount of data on these near-death experiences. Out of the thousands of such experiences recorded a clear pattern of experience emerges: the dying person experiences cracking, clicking, or rushing noises, or sometimes wonderfully harmonious sounds; this is followed by an experience of leaving the physical body – observing their physical body and surroundings from a distance; they then feel themselves drawn through a dark tunnel out of which they emerge into brilliant light. This light assumes an almost personal quality and frequently encounters occur with spiritual helpers or protective beings and the ancestors – friends and relatives who have died previously. There then often follows a rapid review of their life in which they realise instantly where they acted rightly or wrongly. This experience of self-judgement is followed by an entry into a state of being in which past, present and future merge into one reality – a world filled with ecstasy, radiant colours, and immensely beautiful landscapes.

We know nothing more, with such certainty, of the post-death state, for those who reach this realm of beauty are then brought to a being who tells them that they must return to their body – their visit, this time, has been only temporary.

What does this tell us of the Ovate work? Firstly that the realm of the ancestors does exist, and that it can provide support and guidance. Secondly that a realm exists in which our experience of time is transcended, or fundamentally changed. It is to these realms that the shaman travels, to bring back guidance from past souls and insights into the future.

In megalithic times the early Druids were probably not distinctively classed into three branches of learning. The Druid shaman would probably have been the doctor and priest and repository of tribal lore all in one. The bones found in the chambered cairns such as West Kennet Long Barrow near Avebury would almost certainly have been used ritually in the way bones have been throughout the world, to summon the protection of the dead, to ward off evil and to offer augury.

It is the Ovates' particular connection with the Otherworld, with death, which makes them officiants in the rite of Samhuinn – the feast for the departed on 31 October. But it is only in the naive imagination that this concern with death is viewed as morbid, for in reality the Ovate is concerned with new life, with regeneration. They know that to be born they have to die – whether that means in the literal sense or in the figurative sense, as the death of one way of being and rebirth into a deeper experience of being alive.

In working with the processes of death and regeneration, the Ovates' particular study is – fittingly – tree lore, herbalism and healing. The plant world is a great teacher of the laws of death and rebirth, of sacrifice and transmutation, and the tree is the supreme teacher of the mysteries of time, with its roots for the most part invisible in the past and the subconscious, and its fruit and leaves likewise mostly hidden from us in the heights of the superconscious – holding the potential of the future in the seeds that will in due time fall.

The art of healing concerns the application of natural law to the human body and psyche. If the heart, mind or body is out of tune with nature we suffer. The application of natural remedies – with plants, with the four elements, with solar, lunar and stellar power – are studied by the Ovate. Knowing that it is only through death to one state that we achieve a wider life, the Ovate is in this sense also a psychotherapist. The Ovate learns and teaches that it is often only by letting go, rather than holding on, that we truly find what we have been seeking.

How is the Ovate way of relevance to us today? The fact that many healers – of both body and soul, find Druidry helpful lies in its ability to open the self to something more than just the personal. The story of psychotherapy illustrates this point, and suggests that we can place Druidry, and the work of the Ovates in particular, at the leading edge of psyche (soul) therapies.

Psychotherapy as a form of healing began by discovering the value in opening up communication between the different parts of ourselves – within our intrapersonal world. Healing occurred, for example, when our sexual selves were able to relate more openly with our rational cultivated selves; or when our hearts were able to speak freely to our minds. But this was found to be insufficient – for not only do we need to have successful communication between

the different parts of ourselves, we also need effective communication with those around us, in our interpersonal relationships.
Group therapy was born. More healing occurred as we shared our
fears and joys with others – discovering our common humanity and
our unique differences. But more was needed – we could resolve a
good deal of our intrapersonal and interpersonal difficulties, but we
were still haunted by 'existential neurosis' – we needed to move
beyond the personal to the transpersonal, to find our place in existence by going beyond the self. The spiritual psychologies were
born. They opened up the channels of communication not only
between ourselves and others, but also with our overself, our
transpersonal self and with the divine.

By now it looked as if psychotherapists had covered every base
– we had been put back into relationship with ourselves, with our
fellow humans and with our sense of the divine or spiritual. But to
many therapists' surprise the existential neurosis and sense of alienation often continued for their clients, because in all this therapy
they had inadvertently been guilty of 'speciesism': they had ignored
our relations with the rest of nature. We may have successful
communication with humanity and god/dess, but what about with
our home, the earth – with the stars and sky, with animals and
trees? The Druid argument, and the argument of all earth religions,
is that we can only be fully healthy, fully whole physically and
psychologically and indeed spiritually, when we are in communion
with all of nature.

The walls of the consulting room and the church collapse . . .
client and therapist, patient and analyst, confessant and confessor,
walk away from the debris, remove their clothes and immerse themselves in the pool that stands before them in the light of the sun.
Only then are they whole. Only then can they claim that the healing is complete.

We now have an insight into the healing power that Druidry
can bring, and the way in which this can be mediated by the Ovates'
knowledge of herb, tree and animal lore and their ability to
commune with the spirits of the departed. But what of their divina-
tory skills?

Understanding the hidden dynamics of time and knowing the reality of the spirit worlds enables the Ovate to divine without the interference of the rational mind. This mantic work falls into three categories: augury – which is the making of predictions based on signs and omens; divination – which uses particular methods for finding hidden things – whether they be 'intangibles' such as future events or 'tangibles' such as water or metal; and prophecy – which needs no outer methods but which depends on the Ovate's ability to channel higher wisdom in relation to future events.

The methods of augury used in the past were many: from simple weather-witching to sophisticated interpretation of bird flight; from the observation of animal behaviour to the interpretation of planetary configurations. Almost certainly each of the four elements was used for augury, as they were used for healing. It is likely that the signs and associated feelings conveyed by soil cast on a sheet or drumskin were read as a modern fortune teller might read the tea-leaves (or, in eastern Europe, the coffee-grounds), and the shapes of passing clouds or of the images found in a fire or a pool of water were undoubtedly further sources of inspiration. We know the term the Irish Druids used for cloud divination – *neldoracht* – and we know too of more complex methods of divining used in Ireland, including *tarbhfeis*, which involved the diviner being wrapped in a bull's hide to aid their clairvoyance.

> *The Druid took four wands of yew and upon them he wrote*
> *Oghams, and by his keys of poetic wisdom and through his*
> *Ogham he divined that Etain was in Bri Leith with Midir.*
> (*Tochmarc Etaine*)

Divination is a more sophisticated form of augury. It need not be simple fortune-telling – an attempt to see into the future. It can be an effective means of revealing hidden dynamics – whether they are within oneself or within a relationship, or within a group. Divination then becomes a means of gaining self-knowledge and a deeper understanding of the hidden causes behind appearances. Seen in this way it becomes yet another way that we can try to go beyond the surface, to plumb the depths, to look at causes rather than effects. Modern-day Ovates are able to turn in this quest to a number of distinctly Druidic methods of divination, including working with the sacred animals of the Celtic and Druid tradition and working with Ogham, which has come to be known as the sacred tree-alphabet of the Druids. It is claimed that the Druids used Ogham for divination. Medieval Irish stories such as the *Tochmarc Etaine* suggest that this was so, even though actual inscriptions in Ogham, found on stones, have only been dated to the fourth and fifth centuries. Although from the historian's point of view we cannot be certain that the ancient Druids used Ogham, it certainly provides us today with an evocative means of understanding hidden dynamics and future events, and has become an integral part of modern Ovate training.

However, it is not only the divination of the subtle, intangible realms of the psyche and the future that is the field of Ovate study. Divination can be carried out for tangible things – for water and for metal, for items lost or deliberately hidden. Traditionally the Ovate divines with a wand of hazel. Water sources were always accorded special reverence by the Druids – not only were they naturally dependent on a good supply of drinking water, but springs were revered because they demonstrated the source of life springing up out of the body of Mother Earth, and they were seen as access points to the Otherworld.

The Ovates' divining skills would have been used to find water sources and sources of metallic ore, for this was important to the Celts who used both bronze and iron. The Druids, in their capacity as Pheryllt, or Druid Alchemists, worked the metals that the Ovates found in a raw state in the earth. And here we perceive another function of the Ovate – to seek out and find what is hidden. We can surmise that it was the Ovates' function in the past, and can still be today, to find the sacred groves in which the Druids work. Likewise it is the Ovate who finds the wisdom of the spirit, plant and animal world and brings it back for the benefit of all. It could even have been part of the Ovate's work to find criminals and stolen property or missing bodies. As 'discoverer of the hidden', the Ovate might have been the detective as the Druid was the magistrate or judge.

Finally we learn that prophecy was a function of the Ovate. Here the Ovate needed no outer form to help find what was hidden. Their years of training as a Bard, then as an Ovate, their ability to commune with the spirits, their refinement of their being and their attunement to the world of nature meant that at certain times they could prophesy – predicting the future or warning of possible dangers so that they could be avoided. Merlin is seen in his Ovate role when he utters the prophecies compiled by Geoffrey of Monmouth in the twelfth century.[33]

The ability to prophesy should be understood in its widest sense within the Ovate work. The Bard learns how to become open to transpersonal creative energies in order to provide inspiration and integration. The Ovate builds on this connection with the inner world and combines it with an ability to negotiate time-tracks, and thus can also channel transpersonal creative energies. These chan-nellings may take the form of prophecies – in the sense that they deal with that aspect of time which we term the 'future' – or they may deal with hidden levels of reality and causation that require elucidation and communication.

The Ovate curriculum is vast indeed. Just as the Bard needed years of training, so did the Ovate, although we have no details of this from the classical authors. When Druidry went underground with the triumph of Christianity, the Bards suffered the least – they simply pretended to be 'mere' minstrels and poets, all the while carrying the tradition in their hearts and hidden in their words and music. The Ovates undoubtedly continued their work as healers and herbalists – keeping the tradition alive though in a more discreet way, becoming eventually perhaps the Cunning Folk or 'white witches' who acted as local doctors for those too poor – or too wise – to consult the nearest leech, charlatan or quack.[34]

Today, those who study the Ovate grade learn to work with the powers of nature – they learn the Ogham and come to know the trees as living beings with their own medicines and gifts. They work with the sacred animals of tradition, and with different methods of divination, and many begin a study of herbalism or other methods of healing. In particular they learn how to encourage the flow of

Nwyfre through the body. (Nwyfre is the Druid term for life-force, known as *chi* or *prana* in the East.)[35]

The tree which represents the Ovate grade is the yew – the tree of death and rebirth, of eternity. The north is the place of the Ovate, for it is the grade in which we learn of 'The spiritual intelligence of the night' (*The Book of Taliesin*) when we understand the mystery that the spirit is reborn in the place of greatest darkness. The times associated with the Ovate grade are autumn and winter, evening, dusk and midnight – times when we assimilate the experience of the day or the year, and when we are nourished by the great depths of the unconscious.

DRUIDS

Often when the combatants are ranged face to face, and swords are drawn and spears bristling, these men come between the armies and stay the battle, just as wild beasts are sometimes held spellbound. Thus even among the most savage barbarians anger yields to wisdom, and Mars is shamed before the Muses.

(Diodorus Siculus *Histories*, circa 8 BC)

The reason we tend to visualise the Druid as an old man in our imagination is partly due, perhaps, to a realisation that by the time one has undertaken the training of Bard and Ovate one is bound to be ancient! We cannot be sure of the exact time it took, but Caesar mentions that some spent as long as twenty years in their education at Druid colleges. But this is really little different from the time young people now take to complete their education, and Caesar's account is reminiscent of the situation of monastic schools in Europe and as far afield as Tibet, where young people would go or be sent for a complete education: free from the burden of taxation or military service and 'instigated by such advantages, many resort to their school even of their own accord, whilst others are sent by their parents and relations'. Commentators point out that 'twenty years' could have been a figure of speech to denote a long duration of time, or that it might have actually been nineteen years, since the Druids almost certainly used the metonic cycle, a method of reckoning based on the nineteen-year eclipse cycle.

If the Bard was the poet and musician, the preserver of lore, the inspirer and entertainer, and the Ovate was the doctor, detective, diviner and seer, what was the Druid? Their functions, simply stated, were to act as advisor to rulers, as judge, as teacher, and as an authority in matters of worship and ceremony. The picture this paints is of mature wisdom, of official position and privilege, and of roles which involved decision-making, direction and the imparting of knowledge and wise counsel.

We tend to think of the Druid as a sort of priest – but this is not borne out by the evidence. The classical texts refer to them more as philosophers than priests. At first this appears confusing since we know they presided at ceremonies, but if we understand that Druidry was a natural, earth religion as opposed to a revealed religion, such as Christianity or Islam, we can see that the Druids probably acted not as mediators of divinity, but as directors of ritual, guiding and containing the rites.

In addition to this, we know that they fulfilled a number of other functions, which we shall now examine. Separating these out is for the sake of convenience only, for in reality the roles often merged and combined, as we realise when Caesar tells us 'They have many discussions as touching the stars and their movement, the size of the universe and of the earth, the order of nature, the strength and the powers of the immortal gods, and hand down their lore to the young men.' Here we see the Druids as scientists – as astronomers and mathematicians, as philosophers discussing the powers of the gods, and as teachers passing on their wisdom.

DRUIDS AS JUDGES

The Druids are considered the most just of men, and on this account they are entrusted with the decision, not only of the private disputes, but of the public disputes as well; so that, in former times, they even arbitrated cases of war and made the

opponents stop when they were about to line up for battle, and the
murder cases in particular were turned over to them for decision.
(Strabo, *Geographica*)

It is they who decide in almost all disputes, public and
private; and if any crime has been committed, or murder done,
or there is any dispute about succession or boundaries, they also
decide it, determining rewards and penalties: if any person or
people does not abide by their decision, they ban such
from sacrifice, which is their heaviest penalty.
(Caesar, *De Bello Gallico*)

It is natural that those people perceived as the wise elders of the community should be turned to for judgement and arbitration in times of dispute or when a crime has been committed, and some of the most interesting information about the ancient Druids can be found in the old Irish laws, known as the Brehon laws. Irish texts tell us that in 714 BC the High King Ollamh Fódhla formalised the legal system by founding the Festival of Tara, at which every three years the laws already in existence were discussed and revised: and we know some of the names of the more prominent Druid judges of old, including a female judge named Brigh, a male judge named Finnchaemh, and Cennfaela, the Druid of King Cormac, who in the third century AD was said to be the most learned judge in Ireland. Peter Beresford Ellis, in his book *The Druids*, says: 'the Irish system is the oldest surviving complete codified legal system in Europe with its roots in ancient Indo-European custom and not in Roman law, and is therefore the oldest surviving Celtic system of jurisprudence, and one in which the Druids are still mentioned'. Fortunately for us these laws have been recorded – set down in writing as early as the fifth century, according to some sources. Even as late as the seventeenth century some aspects of the Brehon code survived in Ireland, despite attempts by the English to suppress it. Charles Graves, the grandfather of Robert Graves whose book on Ogham *The White Goddess* was seminal in the revival of interest in goddess worship and paganism, was an expert on Ogham and on Brehon law. He initiated a Royal Commission to transcribe and translate this treas-ure-trove of information, which was published in six volumes between 1865 and 1901.

Reading the Brehon laws today offers us an opportunity to enter into the minds of the early Druids – and to many people's surprise, rather than discovering the beliefs of a primitive and savage people, we find a highly considered system that is mostly based upon 'restorative justice' – a concept that is found, for example, on the other side of the world among the Maoris of New Zealand.[36] Restorative justice is concerned with compensation rather than revenge – the offender rather than simply being incarcerated is made to make good the damage or loss they have caused the victim. This picture was marred somewhat in Ireland by licence being given for vengeance killings, but these were allowed only in response to the murder of family members, and limits were exerted on retalia-tion. Undoubtedly we are seeing here an attempt to control situa-tions that could so easily escalate.

As we would expect from Druid law-makers, severe penalties resulted from the unlawful cutting down of trees, with important species such as oak and yew being designated 'chieftain trees' and carrying greater demands for compensation than 'peasant trees'. And when it came to marriage and divorce the Brehon laws were more humane than the later Christian laws. In the times of the ancient Druids, a woman could divorce a man for a number of reasons: if he was so obese that he was unable to make love, for example, or if he preferred to sleep with men, if he beat her leaving visible marks, or if he spread malicious stories about her.[37] Under the Christian post-Druidic law in Ireland, divorce was illegal until 1995 – even if a husband or wife was physically abusive.

The Brehon laws offer us the most complete view of the kind of society that the ancient Druids helped to guide and lead. We have information from Wales too, but the old Welsh laws known as the 'Laws of Hywel Da' were recorded much later than the Brehon laws and offer us less insight into the world of the ancients.

DRUIDS AS TEACHERS

> *A great number of young men gather about them for the sake of*
> *instruction and hold them in great honour . . . Report says that in*
> *the schools of the Druids they learn by heart a great number*
> *of verses, and . . . they do not think it proper to commit these*
> *utterances to writing, although in almost all other matters, and in*
> *their public and private accounts, they make use of Greek letters.*
>
> (Caesar, *De Bello Gallico*)

It is clear from both the classical and the Irish sources that one of
the main functions of the Druid was as a teacher. This involved
teaching at both an esoteric and an exoteric level. Caitlín Matthews
offers the image of the Jewish rabbi to help us picture how a Druid
might have lived and worked. She or he was:

> a man or woman of wisdom whose advice was sought on
> all matters of daily life, one who perhaps also fulfilled a
> craft, one who was married and had a family, one who
> brought the people together for common celebrations and
> whose word was law. Like the Hasidic rabbis who practised
> Qabala and were known as seers and wonder-workers, so
> too, the druid was a person of unusual skills . . . From the
> various Celtic accounts, we find that a druid usually had
> one or more students attached to his retinue or household.
> Again, to return to our Jewish parallel, a rabbi would often
> run a Talmudic school for anything from a handful to a
> number of students. Similarly, druidic students learned
> from their masters and mistresses.[38]

While some Druids may have simply had one or two students living
with them, helping, presumably, with the household routine in
return for training, others gathered around them sufficient numbers
of disciples to form a veritable college of Druidry. In Ulster, for
example, it is recorded that Cathbad, one of King Conchobar's
Druids, was surrounded by a hundred students.

What would they have learned? Just as the monastic orders later became the centres of learning, the Druid colleges, large and small, were in charge of the whole spectrum of education from the teaching of general knowledge to philosophy, from law to magic, from healing skills to the correct order of ceremonial.

We also know that Druids acted as tutors to the children of kings, queens and nobles, and that students would be sent from one Druid teacher to another to learn different skills. Caesar tells us that Druidry originated in Britain, and that students were sent from Gaul to Britain for training. They were sent to the fountainhead of Druid culture – to imbibe at its source: 'It is believed that their rule of life was discovered in Britain and transferred thence to Gaul; and today those who would study the subject more accurately journey, as a rule, to Britain to learn it.'

It is intriguing to think that the earliest recorded systems of education and law in Britain and Ireland are Druidic. When this is properly recognised, perhaps we will see the statue of a Druid outside the law courts in Dublin and London, and murals in schools or Departments of Education depicting Druids teaching within groves of trees.

DRUIDS AS KINGS AND ADVISORS TO KINGS AND QUEENS

There is evidence that some kings were also Druids. The Druid Ailill Aulomon was King of Munster in the first century AD and it is recorded that three Druid kings ruled in 'the Isle of Thule'.[39] Thule was the name given to Iceland, and here lies the fascinating possibility that Iceland was a kingdom once ruled by Druids – long before its Viking conquest. The official history of Iceland states that the first Norse colonisers, arriving in 874 AD, found and drove away a few isolated Irish hermits who had journeyed there via the Faeroe Islands. But recent work on Icelandic blood-group types shows them to have a greater similarity to those of Ireland than of Scandinavia. This lends weight to the arguments of those historians who claim that Iceland had been colonised by the Celts long before the Vikings arrived. This claim gains further support when we learn that the only extant manuscript source of information that we have about the Nordic pagan cosmology, the Edda, was written in Iceland and not in Scandinavia. The manuscript looks remarkably like the early Irish manuscripts of the same period, and it is tempting to see the Vikings of Iceland being persuaded to record their cosmology by Irish Druids, or their descendants.

To return to Britain and Ireland, when Druids were not kings, they were advisors to kings, queens and chieftains, and were accorded such status that they were often the first to speak at official functions. At the court of Conchobar, King of Ulster, for example, no one had the right to speak before the Druid had spoken.

DRUIDS AS SCIENTISTS AND INVENTORS

We know that the Druids concerned themselves with what we term today the sciences. To what degree their mathematics was numerology, their chemistry alchemy, their astronomy astrology, we will never know. But we do know that the building of the stone circles required sophisticated measuring, calculating and engineering skills, and that this same building depended upon a knowledge of the movement of the heavens to such a degree that even the very earliest proto-Druids were clearly skilled astronomers.

The work of John Michell, Sir Norman Lockyer and Professors Hawkins and Thom, among others, shows us that these people were scientists indeed – creating giant astronomical computers in stone. Some writers have even suggested that the Druids might have invented the telescope, basing this idea on the statement of Diodorus Siculus, who said that in an island west of Celtae the Druids brought the sun and moon near to them, and on the statement of Hecataeus, who tells us that the Druids taught of the existence of lunar mountains.

Others have suggested that they discovered gunpowder but, like the Chinese, used it for special effects rather than warfare. John Smith in his *Gallic Antiquities* of 1780 wrote: 'Among the arcana of nature which our Druids were acquainted with, there are many presumptive, if not positive, proofs for placing the art of gunpowder, or artificial thunder and lightning; though like all other mysteries, they kept the invention of it a secret.' We have no hard historical evidence for this suggestion, but it is delightful to think that Druids might have amazed and entertained their entourage with fireworks, as does the Druidic figure of Gandalf in Tolkien's *Lord of the Rings*.

DRUIDS AS ALCHEMISTS AND METAL-WORKERS

While the Druids may or may not have experimented with fire-works, they certainly worked with fire and with metals, and this work was undoubtedly alchemical. Since fire, like water, was and is considered sacred by all those with a spiritual understanding of the natural world, we can be sure that the Druids were masters and mistresses of fire. Their esoteric work with fire is a matter of inner knowledge – for it deals with their ability to relate to and work with the sacred fire within the body as well as within the grove. The fact that the goddess Brighid is goddess of healing and poetry *and* both fire and water provides us with the key to understanding the connection between the inspiration sought by the Bards, the heal-ing developed by the Ovates and the alchemical work of inner heal-ing and inspiration performed by the Druids. Contemplating this one idea reveals the depth of the Druid mysteries, the nature of its teaching and its relevance for us today.

Metalworking in early societies was also considered a sacred art – for upon it depended the tribe's ability to defend itself and to gain food from the earth or from animals. The Welsh tradition states that a branch of Druids, known as the Pheryllt, worked as metallurgists and alchemists in the magical city of Emrys in Snowdonia. This 'ambrosial city' was also known as Dinas Affaraon, the 'city of the higher powers'.

The Druid as metalworker would have forged the swords for the warriors and nobles, which would have been imbued during their casting and annealing with magical spells designed to protect the bearer and ensure them victory.

The sword figures largely in the Druid mythos. It emerges out of the two fixed elements of water and earth in the Arthurian legend:

being pulled out of stone by Arthur, and being raised mysteriously out of the lake when needed. It is born in fire with the skill of the Druid alchemist, and it is raised in the air during the Order's Beltane ceremony, as the sword-bearer cries: 'Behold this sword Excalibur, which rose from the lake of still meditation and was returned to it again. The sword of spirit, of light and truth, is always sharp and always with us, if our lake be stilled.'[40] At a spiritual-psychological level, the sword represents the will. When the will is not aligned to our higher values and purpose it runs amok – and the sword becomes the weapon which maims and destroys. When it is aligned with higher purpose it becomes the sword of spirit – a representation of our ability to be spiritual warriors in a world filled with difficulties which require the warrior spirit to overcome them. In the Druid circle the sword is placed in the south, just as the wand is placed in the east, the cup of water in the west, and the stone in the north.

We can surmise too that the Druids as metalworkers would have cast the sacred cauldrons. Just as the sword represents the 'male' directive qualities of mind and spirit, so does the cauldron represent the 'female' inclusive qualities of heart and soul. And just as the sword figures largely in Druid ceremonial and mythology, so too does the cauldron – representing, at its roots, the origin of the grail symbol.

DRUIDS AS PEACE-MAKERS

Druids and the Druid philosophy have long been associated with the idea of peace. Classical writers such as Julius Caesar and Diodorus Siculus spoke of how in ancient times Druids were exempt from military service and did not bear arms, and how they often pacified warring tribes, passing between the massed ranks of opposing forces urging peace:

> 'For they generally settle all their disputes, both public and private
> . . . The Druids usually abstain from war, nor do they pay taxes
> together with the others; they have exemption from warfare.'
> (Caesar)

Today, every Druid ceremony begins with a call to peace towards each of the four directions. The Druid performing this function faces north, south, west then east, calling out, 'May there be peace in the north/south/west/east'. As the call is made, peace emanates from the Druid circle out into each direction of the world. Finally, all participants say, 'May there be peace throughout the whole world'.

Druids in ancient times worked in sacred groves, and today they still do – whether these are physical ones, or whether these have been created in the inner world through meditation. These groves are seen as places of peace and tranquillity that radiate these qualities out to the world. Druids often sign their letters or messages 'Yours in the Peace of the Grove', and the Order has begun a programme of planting peace groves throughout the world, with the first ones planted in Jerusalem and Northern Ireland.

In the Order we often say this Peace Prayer in our ceremonies:

> *Deep within the still centre of my being*
> *May I find peace.*
> *Silently within the quiet of the Grove*
> *May I share peace.*
> *Gently (or powerfully) within the greater circle of humankind*
> *May I radiate peace.*

We also hold peace meditations on the day of each full moon, and a section of the Order's website is now devoted to the subject, since war and conflict seem to have escalated so much at the dawn of the twenty-first century.

DRUIDS AS PHILOSOPHERS

> *Some say that the study of philosophy was of barbarian origin.*
> *For the Persians had their Magi, the Babylonians or the*
> *Assyrians the Chaldeans, the Indians their Gymnosophists,*
> *while the Kelts and the Galatae had seers called Druids . . .*
> (Diogenes Laertius, *Lives of the Philosophers*, circa 250 AD)

In examining the roles of the Druid as teacher and judge, king and advisor to kings and queens, scientist and alchemist, we must remember that behind each of these functions the Druid was at heart a philosopher. His or her concern was with the meaning and purpose of life on earth, and it was for this reason that Strabo wrote that 'the Druids, in addition to natural philosophy, study also moral philosophy'.

We know a little of early Druid philosophy. A study of the old Irish and Welsh laws, developed by the Druids, can provide us with a glimpse into the ethical foundations of early Druid philosophy. In addition we can turn to the triads of Ireland and Wales, which – although often of disputed origin and clearly influenced by Christianity – provide further material. The classical writers say that Druid philosophy was influenced by Pythagoreanism, and if this is so, we can start to build a fairly comprehensive picture of the philosophy of these forest sages. But the picture does not stop there, because as we have seen in the earlier chapters, Druidry has grown and evolved constantly over the centuries – on its way absorbing or drawing on many influences. In the early days these came from Greece and Rome, and perhaps Egypt and India too. Later, during the revival period, the ideas of the Romantics found their way into modern Druidry.

In the early years of the twentieth century it adopted many of the ideas of the Western mystery tradition, which originated in classical Greece, Babylonia and ancient Egypt. And in addition, until the 1970s, Druidry was influenced by Universalism, which attempted to trace the universal themes in all religions. Theosophy was likewise driven by universalist aspirations, and many theosophists became interested in, and undoubtedly influenced, Druidism.

Into the historic picture we are building, we must incorporate the most recent influences on the development of modern Druid philosophy. In the 1940s and 50s Ross Nichols became interested in the depth psychologies of Freud and Jung. Partly inspired by their insights, he saw in Druidry a way of helping modern humanity reconnect with nature and the gods. The problem of modern civilisation, as he saw it, was that humanity had become alienated from the land and the seasonal and agricultural cycles. In addition, an understanding of the value of mythology had been lost. As a result we had become alienated from the deepest and the highest sources of inspiration. This psychological perspective took into account our deepest needs, and in recent years Druidry, certainly as expressed within the teachings of the Order of Bards, Ovates and Druids, has been clearly informed by it.

In addition, in the last decade or so, Druidry has been influenced by the ideas and philosophies of the holistic and environmental movements, so that alongside its preoccupations with the search for wisdom and union with Deity (who is seen as one with nature) Druidry today is passionately concerned with protecting the natural world, and developing attitudes and lifestyles which promote living in harmony with nature.

In contemporary Druidry, the tree which represents the Druid grade is the oak – the regal tree of wisdom and tradition – the primordial tree that has always been associated with both Druids and the Nemeton – the oak groves where they gathered and taught. The east is the place of the Druid, for it is from the east that the sun rises and from which comes the illumination that all Druids seek. The times associated with the Druid grade are noon and summer – times of greatest brightness and growth.

THE DRUID AS OUR INNER SAGE

The Bard during training has opened to the artist, the creative self, that lives within; the Ovate during training has opened to the shaman who lives within – the one who can travel in the inner realms to explore the fluid nature of time, and the inner power of trees, herbs and animals. The Druid during training opens to the inner wise person, the inner sage who is philosopher and counsellor, who judges and discriminates and who perhaps teaches too.

At present, the only Druid group that gives training at all three levels is the Order of Bards, Ovates and Druids, but it is helpful to consider these three stages or groupings not as a hierarchy, a ladder

we must climb in order to reach enlightenment or full empowerment, but rather as levels of deepening. There is a path, or journey,
that can be taken from one grade to the next, but having reached
the Druid grade the journey can begin again – this time following a
spiral or circular path rather than a linear one. At the Druid level
the injunction is given to 'Generate and regenerate!' To do this we
must die, we must change. The Ovate experience is passed through
– under the sign of the yew we follow the injunction 'Die and be
reborn!' Finally we reach the stage of the Bard and we are able to be
creative, to be fully born in the world, to express our inherent divinity in word, song, art and music.

The three realms of art, nature and philosophy are encom-
passed within the three divisions of the Druid tradition. We are
finally able to unite our artistic concerns with our environmental
and spiritual concerns. The Bard, Ovate and Druid are one person
standing on the earth – poet and shaman, healer and philosopher –
spiritual and earthy.

We ourselves may well not yet be this 'whole person', able to
encompass all these abilities and interests, but the Druid as a model
is always there to encourage and guide us, to shine a light for us on
a path that is not uniform and not pre-determined, but unique to us
and built with our own experience and our own creative genius.

According to your belief and experience you will understand
the image of the Druid as inner sage as a metaphor, as a cultural
creation, as an archetype in our collective consciousness, or as an
actual being or one of a host of beings who exist on the inner planes,
and who are simply waiting for us to turn to them for guidance.

EXERCISE

After reading this chapter, spend a few moments forgetting all that you have read. Make yourself comfortable and allow yourself to come to a sense of inner centredness and calm. Close your eyes and feel all your concerns falling away from you. Focus for a while on your breathing, and then slowly imagine that you are walking through the forest towards a clearing. As you approach this clearing in the woods you notice that it feels unusually peaceful and calm. There is a special atmosphere here. You find a spot that feels just right for you and you sit down, breathing in the smell of the earth, the trees and the flowers, marvelling in the sunlight as it plays among the leaves of the trees high above. You realise why the Druids choose such spots to commune with nature and the spirit, and you decide to imagine that the three kinds of Druids you have just read about as aspects of yourself, come to meet and talk with you, one by one.

First comes the Bard, carrying perhaps a small harp. The Bard sits beside you and you have a conversation together. Ask about your creative self, the Bard within. What does he or she need in order to grow and flourish? When it is time, allow your sense of the Bard to dissolve, and see instead an Ovate coming into the clearing to talk to you, perhaps dressed in animal skins and bearing knowledge of the earth and the stars, of the secrets of animals and plants. Ask how the Ovate can live more fully in your soul. Then, when it is time, your sense of the Ovate dissolves, and you see a Druid walking towards you into the clearing – the personification of wisdom and calm, maturity and clear vision. Let the Druid speak to you and guide you, before allowing your awareness of him or her to dissolve.

Imagine yourself thanking all three visitors and leaving the clearing. Let go of all images, focus on your breathing for a while, then slowly open your eyes, and feel yourself fully present in your physical body – here and now – filled with vitality and health.

CHAPTER SEVEN

CHAPTER SEVEN

THE TURNING YEAR:

DRUID SEASONAL CEREMONIES AND RITES OF PASSAGE

Mankind has got to get back to the rhythm of the Cosmos.
D. H. Lawrence

Since the Enlightenment our culture has projected the message that life is linear – that we are born, we grow old and we die, and that's it. The old message of the cyclicity of life, of life as a circle or spiral, which humanity intuitively knew from the dawn of time, and whose symbols were carved on stones all over the world, was replaced a few hundred years ago by the symbol of the straight line: the male, linear, scientific worldview that, in distortion, worships progress and goal-achievement above wisdom and compassion. One of the results of this change in our collective awareness from a belief in the circularity of life to its linearity, has been a disconnection in the souls of many people from one of the most nourishing of spiritual sources – the realm of nature.

When I met the old Chief Druid, Nuinn, he spoke of a way that had never severed its connection with nature, and which conveyed a sense of the immanence of the divine in all things. In Druidry you communed with Deity in the 'temple not made with hands' – in the 'eye of the sun' – in the open air, in the environment made by the god/dess not by humans. In Druidry divinity was seen as being in everything, omnipresent yet manifesting differently in stone and star, animal and tree. And you communed with and celebrated your oneness with nature by observing a pattern of eight special ceremonies around the wheel of the year – each one designed to help you get in touch with the rhythm of the season, and the life of the land around you.

When I piece together all the explanations that my Druid teacher gave me, often in a café beneath his office in London's West Kensington, I can imagine him explaining the festival scheme, the central observance-pattern of Druidry, to me in this way:

'Take your life and its events. Place them in one line with birth at one end and death at the other end,' Nuinn says, leaning across the table towards me in the café while picking up a knife to illustrate his point. 'And there you have an isolated line beginning in the void and terminating in the void. Other lines might run parallel to yours, collide or cross, but they will all end as they begun – with nothing.' He pauses and looks at me with a shrug, but then says, 'But we know life isn't really like that. We know that death is followed by rebirth because we see it with the rebirth of life in the spring, and – if we are lucky – we remember it when we reach far back in our own memories. So life is like this,' he says, gesturing to the plate, 'Not this!' He exclaims, putting the knife down with a touch of theatre as people start to look at us in the café.

He then runs his finger around the circumference of the plate, saying, 'You are born, you grow old, you die,' bringing his finger back to the starting point, and then again, 'You are born, you are a child, a young man, an old man, you die. You are born, you die,' and so on, several times, until he puts the plate down to allow the waiter to serve our meal.

'What is it that guides the course of this cycle – this circling?' he asks me. My mind goes blank for a moment. 'What lies at the centre of this wheel? What or who is responsible for its turning?'

Then I get it: 'My soul – my true identity that endures through every life!'

'Exactly,' he says, placing a pat of butter in the centre of his dish of spaghetti to mark the place of my soul.

'Now let us forget the individual,' he continues, 'and look at the world. The seasons are clearly cyclical – one following the other inexorably. So we can place them on a circle. That is the circle of the year. But the life of each day we can place on a circle too – it is born at dawn, reaches its peak at noon, and passes from dusk into night, before being reborn again the next day.' He begins circling his plate with his finger, more gingerly now, to avoid the food.

'The circle of the year and the circle of the day have affinities. Winter is like the dead of night, when all is still. Spring is like the dawn of the day when the birds awaken and praise the sun. Summer is like noon – a time of maximum heat and growth. Autumn is like the evening, when the autumn colours seem like the colours of the sunset. So there are the two cycles of the earth harmoniously brought together. Who or what do you think it is that controls the turning of this wheel?' he asks, taking the opportunity finally to begin eating, and also taking great pleasure in the coincidence that now he needs to turn his spaghetti on a fork – which operation he naturally chooses to perform in the centre of the plate.

Again, for a moment my mind goes blank. 'God or the Goddess?' I suggest.

'Well, yes, Deity is at the centre and is the cause of everything. But what specifically causes the cycle of the day and the seasons on earth is the sun. The sun causes the wheel to turn.'

Leaning forward now, he peers at me intently for a moment, before asking his next question: 'And what do you think the connection is between your cycle,' he says, pointing to my plate, 'and the cycle of the earth?' pointing to his plate.

At first I can see no connection – they seem as entirely separate as our two plates of spaghetti. Nuinn circles his plate with his finger once more.

'Birth, death, rebirth. Winter solstice – the longest night. Will the sun be reborn? Yes! And here, opposite, at the summer solstice he is at his maximum strength, at the time of the longest day.' Pointing to the top of my plate, he says, 'Here you are born, incarnated as a spark of light, and there,' pointing to the other side of my plate, 'you are in the prime of your life.' He suddenly grabs the pepper pot and makes a dash of pepper on my plate at these two points, saying 'Summer, winter.' And then two further splashes are made to either side: 'Spring and autumn.' Pointing at each mark, he continues, 'Here we see how the cycles of your life and the life of the earth are entwined. The spring is the time of your childhood, the summer the time of your manhood, the autumn the time of your maturity in old age, and winter is the time of your death. At the centre of the turning wheel of your life is your soul. At the centre of the turning wheel of the earth is the sun.'

He looks around the table for something to use, then with a flourish tosses a spoonful of parmesan into the centre of my half-eaten pile of spaghetti. 'The sun and your soul! Now perhaps you can see why the sun is revered so much in Druidry.'

At this point I experience one of those sudden rushes of insight in which everything seems to come together and make sense in one flash, even though one's everyday mind cannot quite grasp all the connections.

'This is perhaps why someone once wrote that the ancient Druids believed our souls originate in the sun,' continues Nuinn. 'According to this writer, they believed that between lives we go to rest on the moon until our last three incarnations on earth – when we are allowed to rest between lives in the heart of the sun, with those golden solar beings who guide the destiny of our planet.'

THE EIGHTFOLD WHEEL

Such was my introduction to the eightfold scheme that lies at the heart of Druidry, and indeed the Western pagan tradition of which Druidry is one manifestation and Wicca another. Both Druids and Wiccans celebrate these eight festivals, and in fact it was Nuinn and Gerald Gardner who introduced the eightfold scheme and much of the modern versions of these rites into paganism in the 1950s and 60s.[41]

The scheme is based upon the deep and mysterious connection between the source of our individual lives and the source of the life of the planet, and it recognises eight particular times during the yearly cycle which are significant and which are marked by special observances.

Of the eight, four are astronomical events, directly associated with the position of the sun in the sky, while the other four are related to the life of the land and the phases of the moon. If we associate the sun with the masculine principle, and the moon with the feminine principle, we can see that the scheme offers a balanced series of interlocking masculine and feminine observances. The solar observances are the ones that most people associate with modern-day Druids – particularly the summer solstice ceremonies at Stonehenge. At the solstices, the sun is revered at the point of its apparent death at midwinter, and of its maximum power at the noon of the year when the days are longest. At the equinoxes, day and night are balanced. At the spring equinox, the power of the sun is on the increase, and we celebrate the time of sowing and of preparation for the gifts of summer. At the autumnal equinox, although day and night are of equal duration, the power of the sun is on the wane, and we give thanks for the gifts of the harvest and prepare for the darkness of winter.

In addition to these four astronomical, solar festivals, there are four times in the year which were and are also considered sacred. These are the times which were more associated with the livestock cycle, rather than the farming cycle. Since they are not tied to any specific moment in the sky, the day of their celebration is not critical and can vary according to local circumstances. Our geographical location, and now the effects of global warming, can mean that these four seasonal celebrations take place at varying times. In addition, those living in the southern hemisphere need to reverse the dates of all eight festival times, since their seasons are opposite to those of the northern hemisphere.

At Samhuinn, at the beginning of November, livestock for whom there was insufficient fodder were slaughtered and their meat salted and stored. At Imbolc, in February, the lambs were born. At Beltane, in May, it was the time of mating and of the passing of livestock through two Beltane fires for purification. Lughnasadh, at the beginning of August, was the time which marked the link between the agricultural and the livestock cycle – the harvest began and both human food and animal fodder were reaped and stored.

Together, the two sets of festivals represent our complete interconnectedness with the earth, the moon and the sun, and the animal and plant realms.

As we contemplate the festivals over the next few pages we shall see how interwoven is the life of our psyche and of our body, of the planet and of the sun and moon – for each festival time marks a potent conjunction of time and place in a way that is quite remarkable.

Looking at the complete cycle, we shall begin at Samhuinn (also spelt Samhain, and pronounced 'sow[to rhyme with cow]-in'.) Samhuinn is a time which many writers have believed until recently marked the ending and the beginning of the Celtic year in ancient times. This now seems incorrect historically, but nevertheless those who celebrate this time today notice a definite shift in the life of the year – with it dying in some way and perhaps only really being reborn at the winter solstice, the time that scholars now believe marked the traditional beginning of the new year.[42]

Samhuinn, from 31 October to 2 November, was a time of no-time. Celtic society, like all early societies, was highly structured and organised – everyone knew their place. But for that order to be psychologically comfortable, there had to be a time when order and structure were abolished – when chaos could reign. And Samhuinn was such a time. Time was abolished for the three days of this festival, and people did crazy things – men dressed as women and women as men. Farmers' gates were unhinged and left in ditches, peoples' horses were moved to different fields, and children would knock on neighbours' doors for food and treats, which explains the origin of the custom of trick-or-treating on Halloween.

But behind this apparent lunacy, lies a deeper mystery. Druids believe that this time of year has a special quality. As much of the plant world seems to die with the onset of winter, and as the nights draw in, the veil between this world and the world of the ancestors is drawn aside at this time, and for those who are prepared, journeys can be made in safety to the 'other side'. The Druid rite of Samhuinn, therefore, is concerned with making contact with the spirits of the departed, who are seen as sources of guidance and inspiration rather than as sources of dread. The dark moon, the time when no moon can be seen in the sky, is the phase of the moon which rules this festival, because it represents a time in which our mortal sight needs to be obscured in order for us to see into the other worlds. The dead are honoured and feasted, not as the dead, but as the living spirits of loved ones and of guardians who hold the root-wisdom of the tribe.

Next in the cycle is the time of the winter solstice, called in the Druid tradition Alban Arthan (the Light of Arthur). This is the time of death and rebirth. The sun appears to be abandoning us completely as the longest night arrives. Linking our own inner journey to the yearly cycle, the words of the ceremony written by Nuinn tell us to 'Cast away whatever impedes the appearance of light'. In darkness we throw on to the ground the scraps of material we have been carrying that signify those things which have been holding us back, and one lamp is lit from a flint and raised up on the Druid's crook in the east. The year is reborn and a new cycle begins, which will reach its peak at the time of the midsummer solstice, before returning again to the place of death-and-birth.

Although the Bible indicates that Jesus was born in the spring, it is no accident that the early Church chose to move his official birthday to the time of the midwinter solstice – for it is indeed a time when the light enters the darkness of the world, and we see again the building of Christianity on the foundations of earlier belief.

Today, many in our secularised culture really only have one marker for the year, and that is the period of Christmas and New Year. Druidry has eight markers, which means that every six weeks or so we have the opportunity to step out of the humdrum of daily life, to honour the conjunction of place and time.

The next festival occurs at the beginning of February, traditionally on the eve of 1 February. It is called Imbolc in the Druid tradition, or sometimes Oimelc. Although we would think of Imbolc as being in the midst of winter, it represents in fact the first of a trio of spring celebrations, since it is the time of the first appearance of the snowdrop, and of the melting of the snows and the clearing of the debris of winter. It is a time when we sense the first glimmer of spring, and when the lambs are born. In the Druid tradition it is a gentle, beautiful festival in which the Mother Goddess is honoured with eight candles rising out of the water at the centre of the ceremonial circle.

The goddess that ruled Samhuinn was the Cailleach, the Grey Hag, the Mountain Mother, the Dark Woman of Knowledge. But by Imbolc the goddess has become Brighid, the goddess of poets, healers and midwives. And so we often use Imbolc as a time for an Eisteddfod dedicated to poetry and song praising the goddess in her many forms. The Christian development of this festival is Candlemas. For years successive popes had tried to stop parades of lit candles in the streets of Rome at this time. They finally saw that it was impossible to put a stop to this pagan custom, so it was suggested that the populace take their candles into the churches to be blessed by priests.

Time moves on, and in a short while we come to the spring equinox – the time of equality of day and night, when the forces of the light are on the increase. At the centre of the trio of spring festas, Alban Eilir (the Light of the Earth) marks the more recognisable beginnings of spring, when the flowers are starting to appear and when the sowing begins in earnest. As the point of psychological development in our lives it marks the time of late childhood to, say, fourteen years – Imbolc marking the time of early childhood (say to seven years). We are in the spring of our lives – the seeds that are planted in our childhood time of Imbolc and Alban Eilir will ideally flower from the Beltane time of adolescence onwards as capacities and powers that will help us to negotiate our lives with skill and accomplishment.

Beltane, on 1 May, marks the time of our adolescence and early adulthood. Spring is in full bloom, and twin fires would be lit at this time, through which would be passed the cattle after their long winter confinement, or over which those hoping for a child or good fortune would leap. When I was young, the Order celebrated Beltane on Glastonbury Tor. The celebration of the union of male and female is symbolically depicted there in the landscape – with Chalice Well representing the feminine and the Tor representing the masculine principle. We see the same theme in May Day celebrations, when dancing round the maypole celebrates the fertility of the land and suggests an echo of the ritual circle dances that might have been enacted in stone circles in ancient times at this season when the sap is rising.

We have reached the time of the summer solstice, Alban Hefin, The Light of the Shore, by 21 or 22 June (the dates for each of the solar festivals vary each year since the events are astronomical, not manufactured like our calendar). This is the time of the longest day when light is at its maximum. It is at this time that Druids hold their most complex ceremony. Starting at midnight on the eve of the solstice, a vigil is held through the night – seated around the solstice fire. The night is over in a matter of hours, and as light breaks, the dawn ceremony marks the time of the sun's rising on this its most powerful day. At noon a further ceremony is held.

Six weeks later we come to the time of Lughnasadh on 1 August, which marks the beginning of harvest time. The hay has been gathered in, and the time for reaping the wheat and barley is due. In the old days, it was a time of gathering together, of contests and games and of marriages. The marriages contracted at this time could be annulled at the same time the following year – offering the couple a sensible 'trial period'. In some areas a flaming wheel was sent rolling down the hillside at this time to symbolise the descent of the year towards winter, and in some Druid ceremonies a wheel is passed round the circle to symbolise the turning year. The Christian version of this festival is Lammas. (The word Lammas comes from *hlafmasse* – 'loaf-mass' – since bread is offered from the newly harvested grain.)

The autumnal equinox, on 21 September or thereabouts, is called Alban Elfed or Light of the Water in the Druid tradition. It represents the second of the harvest festivals – this time marking the end of harvest time, just as Lughnasadh marked its beginning. Again day and night are equally balanced as they were at the time of the spring equinox, but soon the nights will grow longer than the days and winter will be with us. In the ceremony we give thanks for the fruits of the earth and for the goodness of the Mother Goddess.

And so the circle completes itself as we come again to the time of Samhuinn at the waning of the year.

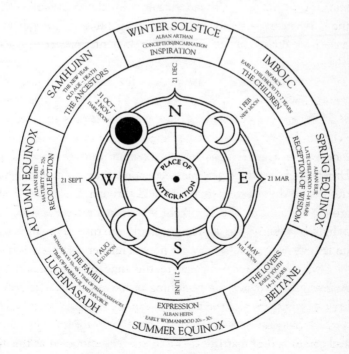

Figure 1. The Druid Circle of the Year

THE RELEVANCE AND VALUE OF THE FESTIVALS

What does it mean to celebrate these festivals? Are we simply trying to revive customs that belong to a different era, and are well forgotten? Those who follow Druidry believe strongly that this is not the case. Just as Christmas and New Year are vital to our psychic health because they give us some measure of the passage of our lives, so the recognition and celebration of these eight festival times helps us to attune the rhythm of our personal lives to the rhythm of the cosmos, of nature. By doing this we find that we develop an increasing sense of peace and place in our world and in our lives.

Let us look at the value of the festivals from a psychological point of view. The four cross-quarter festivals of Imbolc, Beltane, Samhuinn and Lughnasadh relate to key life periods and the experiences necessary for each one of them: Imbolc invokes the purity and mothering that we need in our first years on earth. We need the stillness of Imbolc, of the candles glittering on the water, of the goddess Brighid who sings to us each night as we fall asleep. When we have become young adults, we need the initiation of Beltane – of spring – when the force of our sexuality courses through our blood and when we need the guidance of the tribe and its mythos, not its denial or disapproval.

As we become adults at the Lughnasadh time of our lives and begin to build a family, the rules change – the wildness of youth gives way to the constraints that responsibility brings, and we need an understanding of this as part of the wider scheme of things – not merely a 'knuckling down' to duty with the seeds of rebellion in our hearts.

As we grow old, we approach the gateway to the Otherworld. If we have followed such a path as Druidry, this becomes a time of preparation for the Great Adventure, a time in which we become familiar with our friends and guides in the Otherworld who can show us that death is really a birth to another level – a wider horizon.

If we work with this scheme, we have a chance to invoke each of these phases of our life every year – as if each year were a micro-cosm of our complete lives. In the early spring we open to the child who lives in each one of us – we honour and acknowledge and cher-ish them, and we allow the healing breath of the goddess of poetry to sing gently to them.

At Beltane we open to the god and goddess of youth. However old we are, springtime can makes us feel young again, and at Beltane we jump over the fires of vitality and youth and allow that vitality to enliven and heal us. When young we might use this time as an opportunity to connect to our sensuality in a positive creative way, and when older the mating that we seek might well be one of the feminine and masculine sides of our nature. Integration of the male and female aspects of the self has long been seen as one of the prime goals of spiritual and psychotherapeutic work, and Beltane represents the time when we can open to this work fully – allowing the natural union of polarities that occurs in nature at this time the opportunity to help us in our work – a work that is essentially alchemical.

We move from conjunction to the fruits of that conjunction with the festival time of Lughnasadh – the harvest being that of either children or of creative works. This is a time of satisfaction in our accomplishments – whether that means gazing into the face of our child or feeling the warm satisfaction that comes when we achieve an objective in our field of endeavour. It is at the time of the festival of Lughnasadh that we can invoke the powers of accom-plishment to nourish the need that we all have to achieve some-thing in this world. If we feel that we have achieved something, we can use this time to open ourselves to the satisfaction this brings. So often as we rush through life we do not even pause to enjoy those things which we have around us – our family or home, for example. If we feel that we have not yet achieved anything, now is the time to open ourselves to our potential for achievement. Acting 'as if' is a powerful way to mould our future. If we spend time opening ourselves to the feeling of family or accomplishment, even if we do not apparently have these things, we help to invoke these realities for the future.

Finally, at the time of Samhuinn we can open ourselves to the reality of other worlds, to the reality of the existence of those of our friends who have 'gone before us' and who are still alive and well, though not on this earth. If each year we have in consciousness connected to this plane, when the time comes for our transfer, it will represent a more familiar, if still challenging, territory that we will actively want to explore. Children brought up in this tradition have a warm feeling towards this other realm, rather than being filled with a fear of the unknown provoked by frightening images of 'hell' and unconvincing images of 'heaven'.

We have seen how these four festivals demonstrate a cycle related to the phases of our life on earth. Let us now look at the other four festivals – the solar ones – which represent, at a psychological level, four key functions or processes: inspiration, reception, expression and recollection.

The winter solstice, Alban Arthan, represents a time when we can open to the forces of inspiration and conception. All about us is darkness. Our only guide is Arthur, the Great Bear, the Pole Star. In the stillness of night is intuition born. Both the festival and the function are located in the north – realm of the night and midwinter. The winter solstice is the time when the atom-seed of light, represented both by the one light that is raised on high and by the white mistletoe berries that are distributed during the ceremony, comes down from the inspired realms and is conceived or incarnated in the womb of the night and of the Earth Mother. It is thus a potent time to open ourselves to the fertilising power of the Muse or of the Great Source.

The spring equinox, Alban Eilir, located in the east, represents the time of reception – reception of wisdom, as we face the dawn rays of the rising sun on the first morning of spring. The east has always been associated with wisdom and enlightenment, because it is from the east that the sun rises. And on the spring equinox it rises due east. At this time we can open ourselves to wisdom and the powers that can bring clarity to us.

The summer solstice, Alban Hefin, in the south, represents the time of expression – when we can open ourselves to realising our dreams and working in the arena of the outer world. The summer always seems the time when there is the most energy for getting things done; aware of this, we can co-operate with this energy. We often take holidays at this time, and while it is a good time for active holidays, the restful, tranquil break from the hurly-burly of life is probably best taken in the autumn, around the time of Alban Elfed, located in the west, when the energy moves towards one that fosters recollection – the quiet in-gathering of the experience of summer.

Working every six weeks or so with a psychological process or function or with a life-period is a deeply satisfying experience.

THE DYNAMICS
BETWEEN FESTIVALS

The lines of connection between the festivals on opposite sides of the circle are also worth exploring. The dynamic that runs from north to south, operating between the two solstices, is one of incarnation, manifestation, creation. The inspiration and realisation of midwinter is grounded and given birth in the realm of matter and expression at the time of the summer solstice. The dynamic that runs from east to west, operating between the two equinoxes, is one of elaboration and construction. The wisdom and clarity received in the spring is elaborated and developed by the psyche and is built into its very fabric through the process of rumination and contemplation, inner harvesting, that occurs in the autumn, at the time of the setting sun.

The dynamic that runs from Beltane in the south-east, to Samhuinn in the north-west, is one that is most easily explained with the use of the eastern term *karma*: by mating we create the cycle of birth and death, and we thereby invoke the operation of karma. The joy of sexuality and union is counterbalanced by our fear of death and separation, but both are part of the same dynamic which represents the dance of creation. Both festivals mark processes which represent great adventures – our sexual world is full of mystery and the unknown, of love and the exploration of the depths of feelings, just as is the world of death. Both also represent independence – for we enter our first sexual experiences with an intense feeling of our individuality and uniqueness just as we enter the gateway of death supremely alone. The adolescent who leaves home is under the sign of Beltane and is working with the spirit of independence, just as the dying too are struggling to feel comfortable with being on their own when facing the Great Adventure.

The dynamic that runs from Imbolc in the north-east to Lughnasadh in the south-west is one that is also linked to karma, although here it is a dynamic of dependence, rather than independence, for it represents the relationship between infancy (Imbolc) and the family (Lughnasadh). Both represent times when we are dependent on others, and when we need to attune to the dynamic of dependence rather than independence. Our adolescents and the elderly need help to come to terms with what it means to be a separate individual. Our children and parents need help to come to terms with the strain that having to be dependent on others can bring.

At the centre of the circle – the point at which all these pathways meet – is the place of integration. Here all the qualities and dynamics find their resting place and place of creative union at the very heart of the circle – which is also at the very heart of our beings. In many of the ceremonies this reality is enacted ritually by the Druid moving sacred objects from the periphery of the circle to the centre – thus enacting the movement of integration on the physical level and grounding a spiritual and psychological principle in action.

The centre of the circle represents god/dess and the self; the sun and our soul; the source of all being. As such it is the place where all comes to rest and to fruition.

We can now see how, over the years as one practices Druidry, the circle becomes a magical place in which the circumference represents the round of our daily, yearly and whole-life journeys – inextricably tied to the daily and yearly cycle of the earth, and the eight compass directions with their associated meanings and spiritual and psychological associations. At the centre lies the still point of being and no-thing. The entire space of the circle becomes our sphere of inner working – it becomes a sacred area in which, like a magic carpet, we can travel to other states of being. It becomes a doorway which, like the familiar archway of the Stonehenge trilithons, can give us access to previously hidden realms and altered states of consciousness.

RITES OF PASSAGE AND OTHER CEREMONIES

Nuinn once suggested to me that 'ritual is poetry in the world of acts'. And certainly Druids love ritual as much as they love poetry. In addition to celebrating at the eight seasonal festival times, Druids have special ceremonies for naming, wedding or hand-fasting, and for funerals. There is no 'standard form' for these ceremonies, and they are best crafted to suit the particular occasion. To help with this, Druidry offers techniques, ideas, words and imagery drawn from tradition and from nature, and one of the purposes of training in a Druid group is to learn how to create all sorts of ceremonies from these ingredients. The training programme of the Order of Bards, Ovates and Druids describes over thirty basic rituals which can be adapted and used for a whole variety of occasions – including tree-planting, initiation, birth, death and marriage.[43]

As an example, we can see in the following excerpt from a wedding ceremony, the way that the symbolism of the cycle of our individual lives and of the year has been developed into a journey that the couple takes around the ceremonial circle. At a certain moment in the ceremony, each of the couple – in this case Jane and Michael – are challenged:

Male Druid: Who walks the path of the moon to stand before heaven and declare her sacred vows? (*Jane steps forward*) Do you, Jane, come to this place of your own free will?
Jane: I do.
Female Druid: Who walks the path of the sun to stand upon this holy earth and declare his sacred vows? (*Michael steps forward*) Do you, Michael, come to this place of your own free will?

Michael: I do.

Both are then instructed to walk the paths of the sun and moon (clockwise and anti-clockwise) around the circle, returning to the east.

Male Druid: Michael and Jane you have walked the circles of the sun and moon. Will you now walk together the circle of time, travelling through the elements and the seasons?

Jane and Michael: We will.

Together, they walk hand in hand to each of the four cardinal directions where they are greeted by a representative of the element, suitably dressed, who blesses them with splashes of water, crystals, incense smoke and flute melodies, or other appropriate elemental blessings.

At the south they are asked: Will your love survive the harsh fires of change?

Jane and Michael: It will.

South: Then accept the blessing of the element of fire in this the place of summer. May your home be filled with warmth.

They walk together to the west.

West: Will your love survive the ebb and flow of feeling?

Jane and Michael: It will.

West: Then accept the blessing of the element of water in this the place of autumn. May your life together be filled with love.

They walk together to the north.

North: Will your love survive the times of stillness and restriction?

Jane and Michael: It will.

North: Then accept the blessing of the element of earth in this the place of winter. May your union be strong and fruitful.

They walk together to the east.

East: Will your love survive the clear light of day?

Jane and Michael: It will.

East: Then accept the blessing of the element of air in this the place of spring. May your marriage be blessed by the light of every new dawn.

Having helped to marry friends, name our children and our friends' children, and sadly having helped to bury friends too with Druid funeral rites, I have come to see, over the years, how Druidry can provide inspiration and powerful spiritual and emotional support at these significant times in our journeys through life. Just as the seasonal festivals mark important moments in the life of the year and the earth, so these rites of passage mark the changes and the seasons of our life.

EXERCISE

After reading this chapter, spend a few moments forgetting all that you have read. Make yourself comfortable and allow yourself to come to a sense of inner centredness and calm.

Think about the time of year you find yourself in. Whatever the date is, one or other of the eight festivals will be, at the most, three or four weeks behind or ahead of you. For example, if it is 23 February today, Imbolc would have been celebrated three weeks ago on 1 February and the spring equinox is due in four weeks' time on 21 or 22 March (if you are in the southern hemisphere Lughnasadh will have just passed, and the autumn equinox will be due soon). Focus on one of these times, either behind or ahead of you. Recall the associations that this time evokes, based on the chapter you have just read. Allow your mind to explore these as much as it wishes.

Now remember the same time last year. What were you doing then? Where were you? What was your prevailing mood around that time? Can you see any connection with these things and the particular time of year?

See if you can trace the journey of your life and of the world over that period. What has happened during that year? What have you learned? What have you experienced?

When you feel ready, finish your period of contemplation by connecting again to a sense of peace, centredness and calm, before standing up and stretching.

CHAPTER EIGHT

SPIRITS OF THE CIRCLE:

THE MYSTERY OF OUR IDENTITY

*From the trees Teut draws out many beautiful spirits with healing,
cathartic and defensive powers, whose chief is Esus. Into the stones
Teut writes the records and infuses the messages of the higher worlds.*

Ross Nichols, *The Book of Druidry*

When first approaching Druidry it is natural to think of it as
something ancient – as a phenomenon of the past that we can
examine as we would an exhibit in a museum. But a spiritual tradition
should not be treated like a fossil – if it is to be of value it needs to
grow and evolve, and adapt to the needs of the people and of a world
that is constantly changing. Some critics believe that the kind of
Druidry discussed in this book is not 'authentic' or 'pure' since many
of the ideas or practices have been introduced since the seventeenth
century. But this belief is based upon the mistaken idea that there is

such a thing as an 'original' or 'pure' form of a spiritual tradition: an idea that is no longer taken seriously by historians. Purity is hardly ever a natural phenomenon either; instead, nature offers us wonderful examples of richness – of diversity and plurality and constant change. The idea of searching for purity evokes, as the historian Ronald Hutton says, 'the smell of disinfectant and the sound of jackboots'. So rather than seeking purity or a mythic 'original form' of our subject, we are exploring instead something that is natural and growing, and that is relevant to our needs today, not yesterday.

If a spirituality is presented as a *fait accompli* – an inflexible set of beliefs and practices, however ancient, then automatically we are forced into the position of a consumer. We simply have to accept and follow. The kind of Druidry discussed here, and as practised by groups such as the Order of Bards, Ovates and Druids, takes a very different approach. We see Druidry as a living and evolving spirituality that we can actively participate in, and that as a result is different today from what it was thousands of years ago. We are chefs in the kitchen, working with ingredients handed down to us by tradition and with the spirit of inspiration and our own creativity. We are not customers in a restaurant expecting a ready-made meal.

When I met my old Druid teacher, he had spent years studying mythology – the old gods and the old stories – but he wanted to make his knowledge relevant to the world he found himself in. He had lived through two world wars and the Depression. He saw the alienation of young people from the natural world, and he saw the ravages that industrialisation was causing in the land and in the souls of the people around him. He studied the psychologies of Freud and Jung, and involved himself in social work, and the idealistic youth movements of Woodcraft, Chivalry and the Kibbo Kift. He saw Druidry as holding the potential to bring people back into touch with the land and the seasons, and with the purpose of being alive. He wanted Druidry to draw on its historical roots, but he wanted it to be relevant to people's lives today, and not simply a subject for escapist fantasy or exclusively historical speculation.

I have continued his work and the work of the Order in this same spirit, because I believe that the old ideas can be enhanced and made more relevant to our modern lives if we work in this way. As an example of this approach, which combines traditional and recent knowledge, let's consider one of the most central questions that confront us as human beings: 'Who am I?' Spiritualities, if they are to be of value, need to address this question, and if we combine the insights of modern psychology with the informing ideas of historical Druidry, we discover a potent mixture that can offer much of insight and value.

THE POWER OF THE CIRCLE AS A SYMBOL

In the last chapter we saw how the circle acts as a central symbol for Druidry, representing as it does the cycle of our lives and of the natural world. We have seen how this understanding translates into a spiritual practice, which honours the seasons as it honours our periods of growth and change. Soon we will learn how we can relate this symbol to the old stone circles and sacred groves, but first let us see how this same image, in conjunction with the concept of the 'spirits of the circle', can illuminate our understanding of who we are – the fundamental mystery of the human being.

Jung discovered that the circle represents the Self in the unconscious, and that painting circular mandalas can help towards the healing process of finding a sense of wholeness or completeness in our lives. Within this sense of wholeness, this sacred circle of awareness, he postulated four functions – thinking, sensation, feeling and intuition – which can be equated with the four elements of air, fire, water and earth, and also with the four cardinal directions within the circle of east, south, west and north.

These functions represent what we do in our lives: we think, feel, sense and intuit. But who is doing all this? What is the nature of this mysterious being known as 'me' or 'you'? To explore this further, into the circle of the self we need to invoke what we can term the five Spirits of the Circle – five sources of power that together both influence and actually help to construct the self.

Science currently only recognises two of these, saying that our identity is formed through a combination of genetic and environmental influences. But let us see whether keys provided by the ancient Druids in combination with a modern understanding can provide us with another perspective.

OUR GENETIC IDENTITY –
THE SPIRIT OF THE ANCESTORS

We know that ancestor-worship was a key component of Druidic practice. We can be sure of this because of the archaeological evidence of the megalithic culture – which lies at the foundations of Druidry. Anthropological studies also show us that reverence for the ancestors is a key component in nearly all religious and shamanic practices.

Today we do not worship our ancestors – we may well be interested in our family tree and in the outer achievements of our ancestors – individual or national – but we have no way of, or apparent interest in, connecting with who they were at the level of 'soul-essence'. Here we find the key to a way that modern Druidry can work with the practices of ancient Druidry in a way that is totally relevant to our times.

By consciously connecting with the world of the ancestors, we can draw on a wealth of accumulated wisdom and experience that grows rather than diminishes with the passing of each generation. Druids today see the world of the ancestors not as some shady half-world of the dead, but as a radiant realm which represents a treasure-house of wisdom that can be accessed if you are able to travel there, or you are able to receive visitations from that realm.

Almost certainly the Druids of old, and their predecessors, believed likewise, for that reason placing their burial mounds – the chambered cairns, the round and long barrows – near to the sacred circles of worship. We know from archaeological evidence, that many of the cairns were kept open so that either the shaman-priests or perhaps the relatives were able to visit the burial site and commune with their departed ones. Bones have been found arranged in symbolic ways – showing that they were used for ritual purposes – as indeed bones have been for thousands of years by cultures throughout the world.

How can this understanding be of value to us today? Although lip-service is paid to history and tradition, there is in many people a conscious or semi-conscious belief that once you're dead, you are truly 'gone' – 'dead and buried' – somehow no longer existent. This belief has a peculiar relevance to the environmental crisis we face. We used to believe that once we had buried something it disappeared and somehow ceased to exist. Now we discover that we can't get rid of anything! Waste tips by housing estates leak hazardous methane gas, nuclear tips leak radiation, and the sea harbours vast floating islands of dumped plastic. The same holds true for the dead – though the body decays or is burned, we don't get rid of them! They continue to exist at another level and are often keen to counsel and protect us.

Druidry does not advocate spiritualism in the sense of communicating with the dead through trance-mediums, but it does teach us that we can look upon our ancestors, not as dead-and-gone, but as a rich resource that can provide us with a sense of connection to the world and to the life of humanity. When each generation stands on its own, and doesn't feel connected to its lineage, then we have the problems of alienation and disconnection that are so prevalent today. When we know about our ancestors, when we sense them as living and as supporting us, then we feel connected to the genetic life-stream, and we can draw strength and nourishment from this.

In the Druid circle, the place of the ancestors lies in the northwest – the place of the setting of the midsummer sun and the place of Samhuinn – when we celebrate our connection with this ancestral realm. Symbolically, or metaphorically, we can call this influence on our identity, on who we are today, the Spirit of the Ancestors – a spirit which connects us to who we are as genetic beings. We can sense ourselves and our generation as one link in a long chain stretching far into the past and far into the future.

CULTURAL INFLUENCES –
THE SPIRIT OF THE TRIBE

It is not only our genetic inheritance which influences us and which is a rich resource. We are also strongly influenced by the culture in which we have been brought up. Psychologists, sociologists, anthropologists and educationalists have debated long and hard over the differing influences that our genes and our environment have over us – the debate is known as that of 'nature versus nurture'. Which is the most important? Which has the most powerful impact on our character, our behaviour, the illnesses – physical and psychological – that we might develop? Although in the past some have argued for the idea that we come into life as a *tabula rasa* – a clean slate – to be programmed by society and education, and others have argued that we are almost totally guided by our genetic programming, the most sensible conclusions that have emerged from this debate revolve around different weightings being given to both influences – depending on the individual and the particular physical or psychological feature being considered.

How does this relate to Druidry? Today Druids are aware of the importance of cultural influences, and seek to influence culture in a positive way themselves. It is also likely that in ancient times the influence of culture upon the individual was considered important, because we know – again from archaeological evidence – that the cultures within which Druidry flourished were highly developed. We have the evidence of the stunning achievements of the megalithic culture, with their stone constructions that display mastery of both engineering and mathematics, and we have the evidence of the Celtic cultures with their beautiful artwork in jewellery, stone carving, pottery and metalwork. A reading of the Brehon laws and the reports of the classical authors speak of the cultural sophistication of the Druid system. It was not only the Spirit of the Ancestors that influenced the Druids and those around them, it was also the Spirit of the Tribe which conveyed the cultural as opposed to the familial heritage.

The Spirit of the Ancestors connects us to our individual genetic life-stream. The Spirit of the Tribe connects us to the life-stream of our culture, our tribe, our people. Today we have an interesting phenomenon taking place throughout the world. On the one hand there is a move towards a sense of one humanity, one tribe, one world. This has been brought about, not only by the advances in global communication, but also by the common threats of nuclear annihilation and the environmental crisis. At the same time, paradoxically, we see individual national and tribal groups trying to establish more clearly their unique identity – wanting recognition, autonomy and independence. These two trends need not be mutually exclusive. At one level we need to know that we are unique, separate beings while at another level we need to know that we are one with all beings. So it is with tribes – at one level we need to know that we belong to a particular nationality, race, cultural group or tribe and to enjoy its particularities, customs and traditions. But at another level it is essential that we also know that we are one humanity, one people.

In this understanding, therefore, the Spirit of the Tribe is seen as the tribe of all humanity as well as the particular tribe we may identify with. It is easy for us to feel at odds with this spirit. Cultural conventions, unpleasant experiences of parenting or education, restrictive or repressive cultural codes often make us rebel and live in a different manner or different country from our place of upbringing. Just as we can experience anger with our ancestors for their influence upon us, so we can also feel anger at the way our society has conditioned us. It is important that we recognise this anger and that we are able to say 'No!' to aspects of our ancestral or tribal influences which we find unhelpful or indeed harmful. But having done this, there comes a time when we can separate the wheat from the chaff and turn to the Spirit of the Tribe, as we did to the Spirit of the Ancestors, and ask to be shown its treasures, its qualities. We don't have to accept all that these worlds offer us – we are free to pick and choose. Every society has commendable aspects which we can use as nourishment and to provide us with a sense of connection to the world. If we don't approve of its mores, for example, we may still be able to feast on its art.

The allocation of the different spirits to points on the circle or to the lines of the dynamics that operate between points is not too important, and is not to be taken too literally. But in considering the Spirit of the Tribe, the obvious associations are to the times of Imbolc and Lughnasadh and along the dynamic that runs between them, for it is between the points of the young child and the family that environmental, tribal, influences start to work. Likewise in considering the Spirit of the Ancestors, we can associate this with the times of both Samhuinn and Beltane, and the dynamic that runs between them, since the whole process of incarnation cycles between fertilisation at Beltane and death prior to rebirth at Samhuinn.

THE INFLUENCE OF PAST LIVES – THE SPIRIT OF THE JOURNEY

Those familiar with spiritual teachings will know that the two influences just discussed, and recognised fully by science – of heredity and social environment – do not represent the whole picture that determines who we are. There is another factor which is supremely important, and yet which is not recognised by science, although transpersonal psychologists and certain anthropologists are beginning to research this field. This factor is the influence that our past lives have upon us.

We know that the Druids believed in reincarnation from the classical accounts. Recognising that a powerful influence over us is the accumulated experience of previous lives, we can call this stream of being or soul-essence the Spirit of the Journey. This spirit represents the part of each one of us that journeys from life to life – bringing forward each time the distilled wisdom and accumulated knowledge and experience of lifetimes. For many this spirit lies in the unconscious. For very good reasons they are unaware of it, until such time as it is awoken when they reach that point in the journey when it is safe for an awareness of its reality to emerge in everyday consciousness.

The influence of the Spirit of the Journey could explain why some people are able to surmount seemingly unconquerable obstacles of genetic or environmental origin – how people born with tremendous physical handicaps or in horrendous physical conditions can emerge from them displaying abilities and talents apparently unrelated to their genetic and cultural programming.

Part of the work of Druidry involves turning to the Spirit of the Journey and making connection with it, so that it can guide and counsel us. This is a subtle work which involves great care, for the Spirit of our Journey also carries our personal karma, just as the Spirit of the Ancestors carries our family karma, and the Spirit of the Tribe carries our racial karma.

The genetic and environmental influences will change with each life, even in the unlikely event that we are reborn into the same family stream, and even if we are reborn into the same cultural environmental stream. But the past-life influence represents a continuous dynamic that carries us through each life, and for this reason it is best pictured as an arrow or spiral that rises up, moving from the past to the future, to meet the centre of the circle, which defines our being in this particular lifetime.

THE INFLUENCE OF
THE SPIRIT OF PLACE

It may be thought that we have covered all possible influences on our identity, our sense of self: our genetic and past-life inheritances together with our social, cultural, and educational conditioning. But we need to consider two more influences to complete the picture.

Where we are born, the locality and country in which we live, are powerful influences on who we are and on how we think, feel and behave. If we live in the desert we will be different from the person who lives in the marshlands or the forest. Someone who lives in New York city will have different influences playing upon them from someone living in a village in Cornwall.

The Spirit of Place is of enormous significance in Druidry. In ancient times, although the whole earth was undoubtedly considered sacred, particular points on its surface were clearly felt to be especially connected to certain aspects of divine power. For this reason these special spots were honoured with sacred circles of stone – with avenues or groves of trees, with monuments and with ritual. The landscape was seen as a living temple, and worship often occurred, not in enclosed buildings, but on the sacred earth and before the open sky.

The acknowledgement of the sacredness of the landscape is a central feature of modern Druidry – we visit sacred sites, walk the ancient tracks, attune to the different earth-energies and landscape temples, and open ourselves to the teaching and inspiration that comes when we commune with nature. Hill walking and camping, wilderness trekking and individual or group retreats in places of great power and beauty all provide us with a sense of deep peace and connect us to the nourishment that comes when we feel ourselves as belonging in the world – as children of the Goddess. In the Order today we hold camps three times a year in the Vale of the White Horse in Oxfordshire – an area of countryside that has been held sacred for thousands of years, and whose chalk horse and earthworks bear testimony to the artistic and engineering skills of our ancestors. We also hold retreats on the sacred island of Iona in Scotland – an island that was once called *Isla na Druidneach* – the Isle of the Druids.

The Spirit of Place can influence us profoundly, and such is its tangible power that it has in itself become a term in common use. We know when we have found the right place to live or work. When we experience difficulty in finding our place, attuning to this spirit and asking for its guidance can be helpful. Deciding where to have a picnic, where to place one's bed or personal shrine in a room, or where to buy a house are all examples of ways in which we can open ourselves to the Spirit of Place for guidance.

Each place has its spirit. Think of the spirit that lives at Avebury or Stonehenge, at the Great Pyramid, or in the mountains of the Himalaya. Even the corner of our garden has its spirit, and these spirits all form part of the great Spirit of Place. In astrology, our chart is determined by the time, but also by the place in which we are born, as determined by its longitude. A noon birth in Sydney,

Australia produces a birthchart different from one made for a baby born at noon on the same day in Edinburgh, Scotland. It is the conjunction of a particular time and place that creates the chart and which produces the planetary configurations which influence us. When we celebrate the festivals, we likewise work with a meeting of a particular time with a particular place. Our sacred circle of working, whether for a festival or for individual or group work in a grove, has its Spirit of Place, and by being aware of this, we heighten our sense of its sacredness.

Some people are drawn to working with the Spirit of Place to help purify the environment. There are now groups who pray, visualise, dowse and meditate to cleanse and clear particular areas. They claim considerable success with reduced incidents of crime and accidents in areas worked upon. Dowsers also often work on an area which is renowned for its high incidence of accidents – an accident 'black spot' on a particular road, for example. Here too they are working with the Spirit of Place.

Those who visit sacred sites with intent are engaging in an age-old activity which honours the Spirit of Place. They make pilgrimages to holy sites – and this activity is known throughout the world and at all times – it is a fundamental recognition among all peoples of this spirit and of the necessity to honour and respect it, and to draw sustenance and encouragement from it. In Islam, pilgrimages are made to Mecca. In Buddhism to such places as Mount Kailas in Tibet, and the Temple of the Sacred Tooth in Kandy, Sri Lanka. Hindus go to the Ganges and to Benares while in Christianity pilgrimages are also a strong feature of religious life – whether for healing, as to Lourdes, or for spiritual nourishment, as to the Holy Land, or Canterbury, Rome or Glastonbury. Leaving aside the major religions, we see amongst the earth religions such as Druidry a similar feature – wells and rivers, hills and mountains, burial sites and stone circles, lone trees and clearings in the forest, all these were and are considered sacred and were and are the goal of conscious, dedicatory pilgrimage.

An interesting exercise is to become aware of the Spirit of Place in your room or as you read this book. What does it feel like? What is its quality? Then become aware of a wider area – your town or surrounding countryside. What does it feel like now? What is its quality, its vibration? Then widen your awareness to include the whole country, asking yourself the same questions, before sensing the whole world in the same way. You can even continue it to include the whole universe, for the Spirit of Place can be seen fundamentally as Space itself. Science currently estimates that the cosmos contains three trillion galaxies – more than enough for each one of us to evolve to a position of responsibility for a galaxy of our own. The Spirit of Place is truly vast, for she counts all this for her realm.

In our circle we can allocate this spirit to the line that links east and west – for our sense of space is governed to some degree by our awareness of the rising and setting sun. The east represents those lands which are far distant and from which enlightenment comes. The west represents the 'Isles of the Blessed' – that place to which we go after death, and which is the Summerland, a haven and a place of rest and contentment.

THE INFLUENCE OF THE SPIRIT OF TIME

What else influences and helps to create who we feel ourselves to be? Time. The times we live in represent a fundamental influence upon who we are. Just as 'the Spirit of Place' is sensed so strongly by so many people that it has entered our common vocabulary, so too we talk about the Spirit of the Times, and it is clear that someone living in the twenty-first century is under an entirely different set of influences than someone living in, say, the fourteenth century.

There is every evidence that time was, for both the Druids and the megalithic culture out of which they emerged, an immensely important factor. Many of the stones in the stone circles are positioned so that they act as time-stones – marking the rising or setting of the midwinter or midsummer sun, for example. Groups of stones act as systems for other measurements – for instance to predict the times of lunar or solar eclipses.

One of the likely tasks of the Druid was to calculate the times for the festivals, and the times of impending eclipses. The calendar was considered extremely important, and from France we have evidence of a Druid calendrical system in the Coligny calendar, although scholars are divided as to the degree we can consider it purely Druidic, since it is engraved in Roman letters, leading some to believe it represents the product of an attempt to Romanise the native religion. Dated to the first century AD, it consists of fragments of engraved bronze which have been carefully pieced together to show a system which reckoned the beginning of each month from the full moon (a sensible idea, since a full moon is always noticeable when it appears). Each month was divided into two periods of a fortnight, rather than into weeks. To account for the extra days which always accumulate in any calendar (we use leap years to absorb ours) they had a thirteenth month which appeared in some years and not in others. The names of the months are wonderfully evocative of a time when humanity lived closer to nature:[44]

Seed-fall	October–November
The Darkest Depths	November–December
Cold-time	December–January
Stay-home time	January–February
Time of Ice	February–March
Time of Winds	March–April
Shoots-show	April–May
Time of Brightness	May–June
Horse-time	June–July
Claim-time	July–August
Arbitration-time	August–September
Song-time	September–October

The names of the first eight months are self-evident – from the Seed-fall month of October–November when the nuts and seed-cases fall from the trees, to the Time of Brightness – when the sun reaches its maximum power at the summer solstice in June. Horse-time indicates the month in which people went travelling – in the good weather, and Claim-time indicates the month in which the harvest festival of Lughnasadh falls, and at which time marriages were contracted and disputes presented before the judges. The following month, Arbitration-time in August–September, represents the time when the disputes and claims had been adjudicated and when the reckonings were given. At Song-time in September–October the Bards completed their circuits, and chose where they would settle for the winter season.

A study of the Coligny calendar gives us a good feel for the Celtic people's attunement to the life of the land around them – and of the way they integrated the human affairs of travelling, adjudicating and entertaining within the yearly cycle.

Each of the eight festivals that we looked at in the previous chapter marks a conjunction of place and time, and it marks a special moment in the yearly cycle when the forces of nature are at their strongest in a particular way. At the winter solstice these forces are accumulated deep within the soil – the seeds are fertilised by the reborn light in the darkest hour. At Imbolc the forces of growth begin to be called upward by the sun, and by the time of the spring equinox they are blessed with equal durations of day and night, and equal intensities of earth and sky power. At Beltane the call is to couple and to repeat the inexorable demand of nature that the species might flourish and continue. At the summer solstice the forces of the sun are at their most potent – bringing forth a burgeoning of growth at the time of maximum light and energy. At Lughnasadh, the in-gathering begins, the first of the harvest is brought in, and we accept that the energies of nature are drawing themselves back into the earth in preparation for the coming winter. At the autumnal equinox we sense a continuing of this process – we attune to the setting sun and the golden leaves of autumn, and feel the warm glow of recollection as we survey our lives and our year. At Samhuinn, the forces gather in completely and open out into the Otherworld. Time is no more, for if time was important to the Druids, then No-Time, the world beyond time, was vital too.

How do we honour the Spirit of Time in modern Druidry? Firstly, by working with the eight festivals, and by relating our own life-cycle to the natural life-cycle. In that way we slowly begin a process of reconnection to and synchronisation with nature. That harmony which our ancestors once had with the earth we can build again. Once this new sense of time and of our place within the scheme of time is firmly established during our period of study as Bards, we are able to move on to the Ovate grade, in which we approach time in another way. One of the purposes of working with time is to discover not only how to co-operate with it, but also how to transcend it, or travel within and through it. Why this work should be the sphere of study for the Ovate becomes clear when we realise that it is the Ovate who works with divination and prophecy – both skills which require a particular familiarity with time and an ability to render it transparent.

Time is often considered our enemy – so often we are racing against it – trying to fulfil our seemingly endless commitments within the limitations imposed by the day and its schedule. The Druidic approach suggests that instead of treating time as our enemy, we should befriend it, so that it becomes our ally. In the training of the Order we learn how to create moments in our day or week when we can enter the peace of our sacred grove and move out of time for a moment into the vastness and depth of No-Time and No-Thing. And although it takes a while to learn how to do this, the benefits that we reap are enormous.

In the sacred circle we can relate the Spirit of Time to the vertical line travelling from the winter solstice to the summer solstice – the line that bisects the horizontal line of space. Where the two lines meet – there is the moment of transformation – of infinity and eternity – for the Spirits of Time and Place are manifestations in the physical world of the Spirits of Eternity and Infinity respectively.

If we are keen to be of value, to be of service to the world, we can discover what is needed from us, by becoming aware of the agenda that the Spirit of Time has for humanity and for the world during our lifetimes. Each period of history has had its agenda in relation to the evolution of human consciousness. We tend to think of certain individuals who stand out as great innovators and as agents for the advancement of humanity – but they have become so precisely because they have been aware of the needs of the time and have succeeded in articulating what was already fermenting in the collective psyche.

The Spirit of Time clearly has a powerful agenda for us at the moment – events are moving at an astonishing pace. By attuning to the Spirit, by observing what it is that is needed, and where humanity has reached in its evolution, we can follow the advice of Bernard Shaw, a friend of the old Druid Chief, George Watson MacGregor Reid, when he said: 'Find out what the life force, the creative force, is working for in your time and then make for it too. In that way you become more than yourself and a part of creative evolution.'

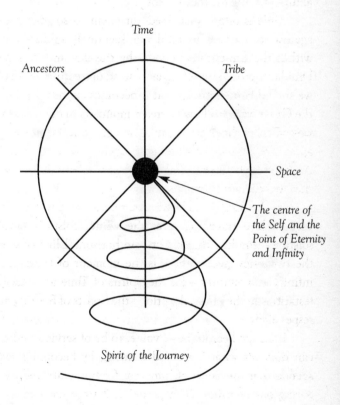

Figure 2. The Spirits of the Circle and their relationships to the Self

THE FIVE FORCES
AND THE ENTRANCE
TO THE MYSTERY SCHOOL

So there we have it – five spirits which are perhaps not really spirits at all in the way that most people would understand the term, although some of us may sense them as mighty beings. Who are we to say, after all, whether or not they are spirits? Is there a being – a Spirit of Time – or are there several: Lords of Time as some call them?

The purpose of working consciously with the idea of the spirits of the circle is to fulfil the injunction written on the portal of the entrance to the Mystery School at Delphi: 'Know Thyself'. By coming to know ourselves better we gain the ability to be self-directed, and feel less driven by forces that we do not understand. In summary, we become more conscious, more self-aware, more responsible. Psychologists have found, through research, that people can be roughly grouped into two categories: those who are outer-directed, who feel that their lives are controlled by outer circumstances, and those who are inner-directed, who feel that they are in control of their lives and for whom outer circumstances are subordinate. George Bernard Shaw provides us with a splendid quotation for inner-directedness: 'Circumstances?' he once said, 'I don't believe in circumstances. If you don't have the right circumstances in life, go out and create them!' If we can come to know the Spirits of the Circle and the part each one of them has played in the creation of who we have become, then we have a greater chance of being inner-directed, and of creating the circumstances we need around us.

Working with Druidry can help us become sensitive to the influence that each one of the five forces has on our lives, and it can also help us to overcome any difficulties we experience as a result of their influence. It would be a mistake to view the rites of the ancient Druids as undertaken solely for propitiation – trying to make peace with the gods of time and place, lineage and environment through sacrifice and offerings. The sophistication of Druid philosophy points to the fact that whilst propitiation may have been a feature of their relationship to these forces, it must also have included attunement and the acquisition of power and wisdom. It is one thing to engage in propitiation as a kind of bribe in the hope that the spirit will not harm you, and quite another to make offerings in the spirit of thankfulness and respect – recognising and honouring a potent force, and hoping too that you will be energised and empowered by them.

Many people are not fully conscious of these forces, which shape their identity and destiny, and as a result their conscious minds are disconnected from the sources of their power. The Druid, however, relates to them as storehouses of energy – acknowledging these spirits and observing their effects, recognising the limitations they impose and their negative influences, as well as the riches and benefits they have given. Druids connects themselves back into the genetic life-stream of the ancestors, the cultural life-stream of the tribe, the power of the earth through the Spirit of Place, the power of the times through the Spirit of Time, and the purpose of their lives through the Spirit of the Journey.

This work cannot be accomplished in a day. In the Order, it is part of the training of the Druid that is undertaken with the method that has been called 'fractional analysis' by Roberto Assagioli, the founder of psychosynthesis, who built on the work of Freud and Jung to develop a psychology that includes an understanding of the spiritual dimension. With fractional analysis we do not attempt to understand, face and integrate everything at once. We periodically face a particular aspect of ourselves, or in this case a particular spirit, and gradually, fractionally, come to analyse and integrate more and more of its riches. In the course of this we move from being at the mercy of the family and culture we were born into, and of our geographical and temporal location, and instead we become increasingly empowered, as we are fed by:

The Richness of Place
The Richness of Time
The Treasures of the Tribe
The Treasures of the Ancestors
The Joy of the Journey

EXERCISE

Which do you think has had the most influence upon who you are today – the genetic influence of your parents and ancestors, or the influence of your upbringing and the culture that you have lived in? Or has the Spirit of the Times had the most formative influence, or perhaps the spirit of the land beneath you? Or is it your sense of your own inner self that has travelled through many lives that gives you your strongest sense of influence on who you feel yourself to be? To get a sense of how you perceive the varying strength of these different influences, try drawing a circle and without too much interference from your logical mind, turn it into a pie-chart, apportioning slices to each of the five influences. Let your intuition guide you to work out the size of each portion.

If this way of understanding your identity appeals to you, you might like to spend some time exploring the gifts of each of the five spirits. Start with the one that appeals to you the most and over the coming days think about the influence it has had on your life – you might want to write about this, or even paint a picture or write a poem that illustrates the part it plays in your life. Notice points of difficulty – with some effort these can provide gateways to transformation. A common point of difficulty has been mentioned already – relating to the Spirit of Time as an enemy. With this, or any other, you could hold in mind the question 'How can I transform this relationship?' Gradually, over the coming weeks see if you can work with each of the spirits, bearing in mind that insight alone is not enough to make a fundamental difference, and that insight needs to be followed through with specific and often practical changes to one's way of being in the world.

CHAPTER NINE

CIRCLES AND STONES, TRACKWAYS AND STARS

Archaeologists for some unapparent reason had been struggling hard for many years to break the popular association of megalithic monuments with Druidism, when suddenly science restored the Druids to their old temple, Stonehenge, wiser and more venerable than before.

John Michell, A Little History of Astro-Archaeology

W e have seen how the circle is a primal symbol for the Druid – representing the self, the wholeness of life, its seasonal cyclicity, its completeness. We have seen how at points around the circle we can station the spirits that influence us, together with the four seasons, cardinal directions and elements, and the eight festivals.

The Druids whose activities are known to us by the records of the classical authors met, worked and taught in circular or oval shaped clearings in the forest – which became their sacred groves. These were known by the Celtic term *Nemeton*. Tacitus in *Germania* wrote, 'The grove is the centre of their whole religion. It is regarded as the cradle of the race and the dwelling-place of the supreme god to whom all things are subject and obedient.' For these Druids, the trees marked the boundaries of their circle, and stored the power generated within it. It was they who stood as guardians of the sanctuary.

The earlier or proto-Druids created their sanctuaries by building circles of stones. For the past eighty or more years, many conventional archaeologists have disputed this claim – rejecting the

Figure 3. Stonehenge, which has been called variously the Great Circle (Cor Gaur in ancient Cymric), the Choir of Giants (Cathoir Ghall in Gaelic) and the Giants' Dance (Chorea Giganteum in Latin)

idea that circles such as Stonehenge and Avebury ever had any connection with the Druids. But as we have seen in Chapter 2, with the revised understanding of the development of Celticity in Britain, it now seems quite reasonable to view the Druid not only as a Celtic figure of authority during the classical period, but also as the representative of a body of religious beliefs and practices that existed from perhaps as long ago as 7000 BC up until the fifth century AD – after which it went 'underground' before re-emerging through the sixteenth, seventeenth and eighteenth centuries. In the light of this understanding, as John Michell points out in the opening quotation of this chapter, a growing body of scholars now accept that the circles were built by the precursors of the Druids of classical antiquity, a group which can be termed proto-Druids.

The stone circles of these early Druids intrigue us – they are powerful and mysterious and call us to contemplation. To understand *why* they were built – their purpose and meaning – we need to look at *where* they were built.

In 1922 a Hereford man, Alfred Watkins, announced in a paper read to the town's Woolhope Society that he had re-discovered an ancient system of trackways, which he called leys or ley-lines. He had found that ancient sacred sites, such as standing stones, circles and tumuli, sacred trees and holy wells, could be connected by straight lines which extend for many miles. He discovered that these often coincided with prehistoric tracks, which were used in those times when people travelled across country, finding their way by walking from one landmark to the next. He found that a notch had been cut into the ridge of a hill, or a cairn had been built to act as a marker, when the landscape interfered with the travellers' view of the next landmark. In time, churches were built on many of these sites, old stone crosses raised, and roads built along the trackways – so that the pattern can still be observed, plotted and even walked by those who are willing to trace the lines on an Ordnance Survey map or to follow one of the guides now available.

But the lines were not simply an early road system. The fact that the connecting points for the tracks were often sacred places shows us that there was not yet a separation between the sacred and the profane. The utilitarian purpose of travelling was still indissolubly connected with a recognition of the sacredness of the earth and of life. The trackways probably originated in the Neolithic period, between 4000 and 2500 BC and seem to have been influenced by a sophisticated understanding of geomancy.

MANIFESTATIONS
OF THE GREAT SPIRIT

Geomancy is known throughout the world and it can be understood as the art and science which determines the correct siting of temples, sacred circles, tombs and monuments in relation to the forces of heaven and earth. It is a knowledge of the sacredness of the earth. One of its basic tenets is that the earth carries currents of vital energy which flows in lines, just as the body carries currents of subtle energy – known to the Chinese acupuncturists as *chi*.

The subtle energy that runs in lines across the earth can, to some extent, be measured. It comprises the electrical and magnetic currents which travel the earth's surface, and the radiations which emanate from underground water and mineral veins. These are the comprehensible sources of their existence, but Druidry points also to another dimension of their nature as manifestations of the life-force, of the Great Spirit. As such, they are conceived as pathways of spirit, and when walked in consciousness can refresh, renew and change us. This is one of the inner purposes of pilgrimage.

All over the territory associated with the ancient Druids – Britain, Ireland and Brittany – at significant points along these arteries of the Earth Spirit, often at junctions where several meet, we find the stone circles. Not only are they sited on leys or at junctions of leys, but they also display a number of other unusual characteristics. Dowsers have always claimed that the circles are located at spots which emit strong radiations, often finding them placed over the meeting points of underground streams.[45] Over the last twenty years, a team of geologists, terrestrial magnetism and earth-science specialists have been researching these sites for more specific information on their unusual characteristics.[46] By 1990 over forty stone circles had been tested with magnetometers and other instruments and they have all, without exception, been found to display anomalous natural energies when compared with their immediate surroundings. All the sites were found to be directly above or very near geological fault lines. This results in an intensification of the currents in the earth's magnetic field at these places.

Other discoveries were made. The granite in Cornwall emits such radiation in the form of the radioactive gas radon that houses in certain areas must be built with diffusers to protect the inhabitants' health. When the stone circles of Cornwall were tested, it was found that they acted as sanctuaries from this harmful radiation, their structure somehow creating a natural barrier or shield. Such a 'sanctuary' effect has been noted by other researchers, but in a different way. In 1972 a zoologist who was hunting for bats at dawn one morning found his ultrasound detector indicating a rapid and regular pulse of a powerful high-frequency signal. He allowed the detector to guide him to the source of the signal, and found himself standing at a megalithic site without a bat in sight.

The Institute of Archaeology at Oxford followed up the zoologist's observation, finding significant patterns of ultrasound at several sites with standing stones.[47] They were strongest at dawn each day, but rose to a particularly powerful emission that lasted for several hours on the mornings of the spring and autumn equinoxes.

In addition to this ability of certain standing stones to sound out a note, albeit inaudible to our ears, the Oxford research also discovered that a stone circle, such as Stonehenge, could also sometimes act as an ultrasonic barrier – creating complete ultrasonic silence within the circle. Again we see the circle as a place of sanctuary, as a place in which we can go to find peace and silence within.

THE DRUID STAR WISDOM

Being located at places of unusual power on the earth's surface is only half the reason why stone circles are where they are, and why they were built in their particular way. At the beginning of the last century Sir Norman Lockyer, the astronomer and scientist and founder of *Nature* magazine, initiated the study of stone circles for their astronomical orientations. On holiday in Greece, he remembered that churches were traditionally orientated towards the point of sunrise on the feast day of their patron saint, and he decided to see whether orientation was a significant factor in the Greek temples he was visiting. His researches intrigued him and led to his determination to study the orientation of the older structures of Egypt. He travelled there in 1891 and discovered that the temple of Amon-Ra at Karnak faced the setting sun of the midsummer solstice – not in his day, but by calculation, in about 3700 BC, when the last rays of the sun would have entered the inner sanctuary at the end of the temple avenue.

The orientation of Stonehenge towards the midsummer sunrise and the midwinter sunset was already well known – both events being visible from the centre of the circle through the narrow stone gateways of the trilithons. This led Lockyer to research Stonehenge and other megalithic sites, resulting in his publication of *Stonehenge and other British Stone Monuments Astronomically Considered* in 1906. The main conclusion that he drew from his research was that the earliest sites were laid out to mark sunrise or sunset at the times of the old Celtic cross-quarter day festivals discussed in Chapter 7. Sometimes the sites would indicate the transit of 'warning' stars that signalled the sun's appearance at these times.

This fact in itself is strong evidence for the idea that the Celtic Druids received their knowledge from the earlier proto-Druids – the megalithic builders – since the very stones themselves show that these pre-Celts were honouring those special times of the year which later continued to be recognised by Celtic society, and later still, by co-option, even by Christianity. Lockyer also found that later constructions were oriented to mark the solstices – by about 1600 BC this had become the general practice among the circle builders.

Lockyer initiated an impulse to study the astronomical orientations of stone circles which was taken up by, among others, the astronomer Gerald Hawkins of Boston University. In 1965 Hawkins published *Stonehenge Decoded*, in which he detailed his discovery that by computing the extreme seasonal positions of the sun and moon in 1500 BC ten of the sighting lines and stone alignments of the monument pointed to solar positions and fourteen to lunar ones. He also proposed the idea that the fifty-six Aubrey holes at Stonehenge were used to mark the fifty-six years of the moon's eclipse cycle. The archaeologist Professor Atkinson attempted to debunk the idea that Stonehenge could have been constructed with these sophisticated functions in mind, but was converted to astro-archaeology, as it has come to be called, after studying the work of Professor Alexander Thom.[48] An engineer, Thom had made accurate surveys of several hundred circles and megalithic sites all over Britain. In studying these surveys, he came to the conclusion that they were all meticulously designed according to a unified standard or canon of geometry that seemed closely related to the system of mathematics that we know as Pythagorean.

Since Pythagoras taught over a thousand years after the construction of these sites, it seems that the claim made by Clement of Alexandria in the second century that Pythagoras learned his science and philosophy from the Druids, rather than vice versa, may not be so unlikely after all. There is a Druid adage that the truth is 'written in the stones'. It seems that the astro-archaeologists have at last begun to decipher this writing that has remained incomprehensible for so long.

In addition to apparently knowing the secrets of Pythagorean geometry, all the classical writers agree that the Druids were well versed in a knowledge of astronomy. Pomponius Mela tells us that they knew 'the movements of the heavens and of the stars', and that they understood the relationship between the moon and the tides. The writer Jordanes quotes a lost work of the fifth century, which refers to a wise man called Dicenus who lived in the first century, and whom scholars believe was probably a Druid. Of his tribe it was said that they knew, in addition to the names of 365 stars, 'the course of the twelve signs of the zodiac, and of the planets passing through them and the whole of astronomy'. This statement is substantiated by the fact that when Dicenus was said to be living, the Coligny calendar was in use in Gaul, and as Beresford Ellis says in *The Druids*: 'Produced before the Roman conquest of Gaul, this calendar is far more elaborate than the rudimentary Julian calendar and has a highly sophisticated five-year synchronisation of lunation with the solar year. It is a masterpiece of calendrical calculation and a practical demonstration of the proof of Cicero's claim as to the astronomical ability of the Druids.'

Today, Druids will often practise or study astrology, combining conventional Western astrology with their understanding of Druid star lore, and some astrologers have developed Celtic astrological systems, building on the association of the sacred trees with the lunar months alluded to in modern times by Robert Graves.[49]

To return to a consideration of the stone circles, some commentators have assumed that they were used as observatories – Neolithic astronomical computers that were used to predict lunar eclipses and to indicate the correct times for festivals and for sowing and harvesting. But to see them in this way is to understand only a small part of their purpose. Knowing that they were orientated with reference to the sun, moon and certain stars, and that they were laid out with an understanding of sacred geometry, we need then to remember that they were positioned at key points on the energy system of the earth. Their location on leys and at ley junctions combined with their orientations to the heavens rendered them able to act as 'receiving stations' for direct influences from heavenly constellations especially at certain seasons of the year. Ceremonies performed there would be immensely powerful when the Spirit of Time united with the Spirit of Place within a sanctuary created not only by the underlying geology and overarching constellations, but also by the fact that the leys, the arteries, of the Earth Spirit could both bring power to the site and also distribute the power generated there across the land.

The men and women who built and worked with these circles were clearly remarkable people. Not only did they accomplish the engineering feats necessary for their construction, but they performed these within the constraints of a sophisticated geometry and science of measurement.[50] This they combined with an understanding of energy fields to determine each circle's location, and with an understanding of astronomy to determine the siting of its individual stones.

The stones themselves were chosen with great care – often necessitating lengthy journeys from quarry to site (even when different types of stone were closer to hand but clearly deemed unsuitable). These early builders understood the different qualities of stone in ways that we are only just beginning to comprehend. We now know, for instance, that quartz rocks attract and store earth magnetism and electricity, and this would explain why many of the stone circles include stones with quartz.

THE POWER OF
SOUND AND LIGHT

As if the capacities of the early Druids already outlined were not enough, they showed an ability with their building of these circles to create sanctuaries of silence, wombs of timelessness surrounded by time-marking stones, and an ability to use the play of light and shadow – of sunlight and moonbeams – in a way that marks them out as our culture's first theatrical lighting designers and technicians. It must have been immensely dramatic for the Druid initiate to witness the sun rising between the trilithons at Stonehenge, or entering the inner sanctuary at New Grange in Ireland at the winter solstice – the finger of the dawn ray gradually illuminating the rear chamber. The builders of the circles and tumuli knew that light and shadow were profoundly important, not only in the way that human consciousness can be affected by the drama of these natural phenomena, but also because they represent the two aspects of duality which are in fact one: out of darkness is born the light and without light we could not comprehend its opposite, darkness. In the chamber of the New Grange tumulus the candidate for initiation would have waited in total obscurity within the womb of the earth at the time of the longest night of the winter to experience a ritual rebirth as the dawn rays of the rising midwinter sun pierced the back of the chamber, heralding the rebirth of the year.

Recent work has revealed the unusual acoustic properties of some megalithic monuments. Certain chambers, such as at New Grange, produce 'standing waves' of sound, and some researchers now believe that rituals within these chambers would have utilised these acoustic effects to enhance the sound of their chanting and drumming.[51]

THE SONGS OF OUR ANCESTORS ARE ALSO THE SONGS OF OUR CHILDREN

No stone circles were built after 1000 BC. We can find a number of reasons for this. There are remains of over a thousand circles to be found in Britain and Ireland. Bearing in mind that many have been destroyed by farmers clearing land, or Christians removing pagan idols, we can assume that by 1000 BC there must have been many more than the one thousand now extant. It is therefore conceivable that, as saturation level was reached, the motive to build any more began to diminish. It is unlikely, however, that this was the only or even the real reason for the circles' demise. Climatic changes at this time had begun to force people off marginal land and the resulting competition for agriculturally fertile territory resulted in strife and instability, forcing communities to turn away from constructing or expanding stone circles and instead to create defensive structures and manufacture weapons. As an example of this, we can see evidence that the expansion of the Stonehenge complex ceased at about the turn of the millennium when construction work on a great two-mile earthwork-flanked avenue came to an abrupt halt.

The 'classical' Druids, whose existence only began to be recorded in the first century BC, met in sacred groves and not in stone circles. The sacred circle was moved from the guardianship of stones to that of trees. Whether or not the old stone circles were ever used by these Druids we may never know, but as Revival Druidry gained momentum, the circles began to be used once again by Druid groups from the nineteenth century onwards, and new stone circles are now built every year in Britain, sometimes in conjunction with camps and workshops to explore the metaphysics and engineering involved in their construction. Today, if you unexpectedly come across a stone circle, it could be ancient or it could be very new. Perhaps the best known of these new circles is on the farm used each year for the Glastonbury music festival – symbolising perfectly the way in which these archetypal symbols from our ancient past appeal to young people today and are now being reborn. Truly 'the songs of our ancestors are also the songs of our children'.[52]

EXERCISE

As an exercise in relation to this chapter, you might like to visit a stone circle. When you arrive, before entering the circle spend a few moments calming yourself and coming to a sense of centredness before calling to mind the ideas about circles presented in these pages. Every stone circle has its inner or spirit guardian, and it is wise to silently ask this guardian if you might enter their sacred space. Unless you feel an intuition or a message not to proceed, become fully aware of yourself being outside the circle, and then in full awareness step into the circle. Walk respectfully within it, and find a spot to attune to the energy of the place. How does it feel? Does it feel different inside as opposed to outside the ring of stones? What is the quality of energy here? Guided by your intuition, touch the stones, if you like, to feel their power, but remember that some stones (more usually single standing stones) were placed to draw power down into the earth to increase its fertility, and if you touch such a stone for too long you may feel drained of energy, because it was sited to absorb rather than radiate power. Most stones, however, will invigorate you. Finally, give thanks to the guardian of the circle, and in full consciousness, step out of the circle, and notice if you feel different.

CHAPTER TEN

DRUID TREE LORE

Trees in particular were mysterious, and seemed to me
direct embodiments of the incomprehensible meaning of life.
For that reason, the woods were the place that I felt closest
to its deepest meaning and to its awe-inspiring workings.

C. G. Jung, *Memories, Dreams, Reflections*

As we have seen from the etymology given in the first chapter,
Druids were wise men and women of the trees. One of the
world's largest tree-planting movements is called The Men of the
Trees and was started by a Druid, the late Richard St Barbe Baker.[53]
Probably few of its members realise that he based the name of his
movement on one meaning of the word 'Druids'.

One of the reasons why the subject of the Druids fascinates us
is because there is such a strong association between them and trees.
If we close our eyes and imagine a Druid, we will often see them
beside a tree, or within a sacred grove of trees. We sense that Druids

were at one with nature in a way that we no longer are – and those of us who aspire to become Druids do so because we want to attain that at-one-ness, that union, for ourselves. In a conscious way we recognise the beauty of trees and their value to us, but just below the surface of our consciousness lies the knowledge that trees also possess keys and powers that, if we were to share in them, would enrich our lives immeasurably.

OGHAM – THE TREE ALPHABET OF THE DRUIDS

Druids today use a particular method for communicating and remembering their wealth of tree-knowledge. This is known as the Ogham (which means 'language' and is pronounced o'um, or och'um). It consists of twenty-five simple strokes centred on or branching off a central line. It is similar in purpose, but separate in origin, from the Nordic runes. The Ogham characters were inscribed on stones and probably on staves of wood. As a method of writing it is laborious, but as a language of symbolism it is powerful. Its origins are lost in the mists of time, and most of the existing inscriptions have been dated to only the fifth and sixth centuries, but whether originally Celtic or pre-Celtic we may sense that it carries with it some of the very earliest of Druid wisdom. Amongst our sources of information about its use are, from Ireland, the twelfth-century *Book of Leinster*, the fourteenth-century *Book of Ballymote* and O'Flaherty's *Ogygia*, published in 1793. From Scotland, transcribed from the oral tradition in the seventeenth century, we have *The Scholar's Primer*. But it was the poet Robert Graves who, following in the footsteps of his grandfather, an Ogham expert, brought this arcane system into public awareness once again with his publication of *The White Goddess* in 1948.

Each stroke of the Ogham corresponds to a letter of the alphabet. This letter represents the first letter of the tree allocated to it – so that the sign ⊦ represents the letter B, and the tree beith, the birch. The sign ⊨ represents the letter L, and the tree luis, the rowan, and so on.

Although we know the letters that each stroke represents, and can translate the ancient Ogham inscriptions accordingly, we cannot be so confident when we come to associate the trees with particular months, as suggested by Robert Graves. There has been much controversy as to whether the Ogham really was used, as Graves asserts, as a calendar by the Druids – linking thirteen of the trees and letters of the alphabet to the lunar months. Whilst it is important to be aware that there is controversy, it is also important to understand that Druidry is evolving, and that if Druids didn't correlate them thousands of years ago, many do now. If it was Robert Graves' invention, then he was acting as a Druid at the time – he was inspired, in other words. Someone has to invent things, or 'receive' them from the Otherworld, and just because he or she does so in AD 1948 rather than 1948 BC is in the final analysis unimportant to those of us who want to use Druidry as a living system, as opposed to those who want to study its origins for a purely academic purpose.

The essential point about the Druid use of Ogham is this – it provides a system that can be used in the same way as the Tree of Life of the Qabalists. Whereas the Qabalists use one tree, the Druids use a grove, a wood – filled with many trees and woodland plants. By clearly building up this wood in the imaginal world and by then associating each tree or plant with a different number, god or goddess, animal, bird, colour, mineral, star, divine or human principle, the Druid is able to retain mentally far more information than could be learned by rote. This use of an image as a mnemonic (memory aid) is well known as an esoteric discipline through the ages. The ancient Greeks, for example, visualised a theatre – each part of which was associated with an item that needed remembering.

But to see the Druid use of Ogham simply as a mnemonic for storing data is to fail to recognise its true purpose and value, for, having 'peopled the forest' – having learned the associations – the Druid is then able to use this network of data in just the same way that a computer can work on stored data to produce numerous combinations and recombinations. The associations start to interrelate and cross-fertilise of their own accord at an unconscious level.

The method of free association used in psychoanalysis can provide a glimpse into the secret world of connections and associations that are made in the unconscious, and the particular contribution of esoteric disciplines is in providing a framework that exists partly in the conscious mind, but which, like a tree whose roots are invisible to us, is also immersed in the unconscious – allowing both aspects of the self to feed from it and to nourish it. In other words, if you build a grove of trees in the imagination, or a 'Tree of Life' if you are a Qabalist, you create a structure which operates not only in the conscious waking self, but also in the unconscious, attracting to it associations, ideas, images and experiences. In this way it acts as a bridge between these two parts of the self. At a deeper level the creation of such a structure allows the influx of transpersonal energies into the personal or individual psychic system in a way that is safe and structured because the channels for its reception and integration have already been built.

One of the most extraordinary things to contemplate is that as we think and make associations, our brains actually make connections and grow physically. The more we use our brain, the more dendrites (the 'arms' between brain cells) are grown, and the more synaptic connections are made (connections from the end of one dendrite to another). These neural pathways are called dendrites because they look like the branches of a tree, and *dendrite* is Greek for 'tree-like'. Photographs of sections of the cerebral cortex look like photos of a thicket of trees in winter. One of the first tasks that we undertake when we begin training in the Order of Bards, Ovates and Druids is to create an inner sanctuary for meditation – a sacred grove of trees in our imaginations. Once this is well established in our minds, we can develop it over many months to create a network of associations, and as we do this we are literally building a thicker, richer complex of connections at a physical level in our brains, as well as a structure on a subtler level in the psyche which can connect our conscious self with our unconscious self, and – ultimately – with the Otherworld.

SACRED TREES AND PLANTS

Druids view all trees and plants as sacred, but the Ogham singles out twenty-five trees and plants for our attention. Each of these is linked with a character of the Ogham script, with a letter of the alphabet and with a particular period during the year.

There is a certain amount of controversy over the association of some of the Ogham characters with certain of the trees, and some authors have chosen different ways of associating them with the times of the year. Those who are interested in following the intricacies of these arguments can do so by studying the relevant literature.[54] But it is important to understand that no one list is absolutely and definitely the true or correct list of sacred trees – although about many there is no disagreement. Most of the controversy revolves

Letter	Irish name	Tree
B	beith	birch
L	luis	rowan
F	fearn	alder
S	saille	willow
N	nuinn	ash
H	huathe	hawthorn
D	duir	oak
T	tinne	holly
C	coll	hazel
Q	quert	apple
M	muinn	vine
G	gort	ivy
NG	ngetal	broom/fern
STR	straif	blackthorn
R	ruis	elder
A	ailm	fir/pine
O	onn	gorse
U	ur	heather
E	edhadh	aspen
I	ido	yew
EA	ebhadh	aspen
OI	oir	spindle
UI	uileand	honeysuckle
IO	iphin	gooseberry
(AE)	phagos	beech

Figure 4. The Ogham Alphabet

around the allocation of the trees to the months, and since we have no physical proof of how or whether the early Druids made these connections, it seems important to allow our inner senses to guide us, and to be aware of the fact that writers disagree. The best approach is to establish our own personal relationship with the trees and their spirits. If we fill ourselves with other people's ideas about which trees are sacred and what properties they possess or symbolise, it tends to block our own intuitive impressions. After we have spent some time working with trees in ways that are outlined in the Ovate work, we can then turn to the different authors and see whether their insights and allocations are helpful or misleading for us.

Whilst the way that we come to a knowledge of the powers and qualities of the trees cannot be taught in a book, since it involves work outside in contact with living trees, and within one's own sacred grove, we will look at some of the attributes of three trees and one sacred plant, to give an insight into their value as part of modern day Druidry.[55]

BEITH – THE BIRCH TREE

The Bardic school or grade is symbolised by the birch tree. It is the first tree in the Ogham cipher, and as such represents the number 1. This is fitting, for it is the birch that we plant first on virgin land if we want to create a wood or forest. It is known, for this reason, as the pioneer tree, and it can be seen also as the tree which helps to birth the forest. So it is a tree of birth – an appropriate tree to symbolise the first level of Druid working, when we are born into this new way of seeing and knowing.

The Ogham can also be used for divination, and when we draw the card, or throw the disc or stave of the birch, we know that this signifies new beginnings for us, and – depending on its relative position in the spread – we know that we must either pioneer a new endeavour or that something is being born in our lives. Often, before we can give birth to the new, we need to cleanse ourselves of the old. Again, the birch tree is an appropriate symbol for this process of purification in preparation for new beginnings. In Scandinavia, switches of birch are used on the body to stimulate the process of purification in the sauna, and can be used in Druid sweat-house rituals too. In Britain the birch rod was used rather more ferociously to purify criminals of their misdeeds, and earlier still in an attempt to expel evil spirits from 'lunatics'. In some areas it was customary to drive out the spirits of the old year with birch switches, and throughout Europe birch twigs were used for 'beating the bounds'.

So to prepare for the new, we must free ourselves of the debris of the old, and birch can help us do this, and can point the way forward, for when we are lost in the forest, the shining whiteness of the birch trunk leads us onward – it offers guidance and orientation in the darkness of our journey. The very word 'birch' derives from a root meaning 'bright' or 'shining' in nearly all languages with Indo-European origins.

Robert Graves allocates this tree to a month stretching from 24 December to 20 January, using a calendar of thirteen months, since both Caesar and Pliny reported that the Druids divided their year into lunar months. He chooses as the first month that which follows the winter solstice – when the year is reborn, and the days begin to lengthen.

As with much of this work, one finds that other traditions hold many things in common. The shaman of the Siberian Gold Eskimos climbs a birch tree at the high point of an initiation ceremony, circling its trunk nine times. The Buryat and the central Asian Altai shamans carve nine notches in the trunk of a young birch – representing the steps they must take to ascend to heaven. The birch shares with the ash the distinction of being used as a representative of the Cosmic World-Tree – the *Axis Mundi*. This tree links the Underworld with Middle Earth and Heaven above. The shaman climbing the birch uses it as a sky-ladder to symbolise his ability to visit other worlds.

In Britain the birch was often used for maypoles – our version of the *Axis Mundi* around which we turn and turn. And at the same season it was the twigs of birch that were used for kindling the Beltane fire. Birch was also used to make babies' cradles, for if birch could drive evil from the old year, and from lunatics and criminals, it could ward off ill for the newborn too. And since birch is the tree of birthing the new, what other wood is more fitting for the newly born?

IOHO – THE YEW TREE

As we approach the heart of the Druid mystery, we enter the grove of the Ovates. The tree of the Ovates is the yew.

We associate the yew tree with death – in Britain they grow in our graveyards, and the dark green spikes of this evergreen are deadly poison. It is likely that the Latin name for this tree, *taxus*, is the root for the word toxic. This connection with death is significant in the Druid understanding of the yew – for whereas the Bardic grade allowed us to be reborn into a new world of understanding and expression under the sign of the birch, as we enter the Ovate grade we come to an experience of symbolic death.

But of course death is merely a gateway into greater life, a letting go in order to be reborn to a new level – and this is what is signified in the Ovate work. The yew tree, seen in this way, is the tree of both death and rebirth, and as such becomes the tree of eternity. The yew, certainly for mortal man, appears to be eternal – it can live for over two thousand years, and its guardianship of the graveyard symbolises the eternal life that is always with us, even when we are separated from our transient body. It signifies the mystery of transcendence over time, and whereas in the Bardic grade we worked with the central scheme of Druidry which defined the relationship of time and space within the mandala of the human and earthly cycles, in the Ovate grade we travel beyond and through this frame of reference to approach the heart of timelessness.

One of the reasons for the longevity of the yew lies in the ability of its branches to grow down into the ground to form new stems which grow to become trunks of separate but linked growth. Although the central trunk becomes old and decays within, a new trunk grows inside this and eventually cannot be distinguished from the original. Because of this extraordinary method of self-renewal, the yew tree symbolises the mystery of self-transformation, renewal and rebirth – the mystery that in age we are youthful, in youth we are age-old, and that the source of our life brings perpetual renewal.

Robert Graves places the yew on the last day of the year, at the eve of the winter solstice, at the time of the year's death before being reborn at the solstice time itself. Liz and Colin Murray, in *The Celtic Tree Oracle*, differ from Graves, placing the yew at the time of Samhuinn. In the Druid ceremony at this time a sprig of yew is distributed to each participant, indicating the yew's relationship to this time of year, our ability to commune with those who have gone before us, and our need for renewal and connection to the qualities of both release and timelessness. Drawing this card or sign on a disc or Ogham stave in divination can indicate that we, or the issue in question, need to enter a period of death, of letting go in order for renewal to occur.

DUIR – THE OAK TREE

With the oak we come to the central circle of the threefold Druid initiation. The oak represents the Druid not only because the word Druid may well derive from words for the oak, making the Druid the one with 'knowledge (*wid*) of the oak (*dru*)', but also because the oak represents the tree of tradition in Druidry.

The associations to the oak are many – it is king or queen of the forest – venerable in both age and form. The oak tree is often struck by lightning – signifying its ability to attract the energy, inspiration and illumination of the sky father or of the thunder-god Taran. He who has knowledge of the oak has knowledge of the power of the elements and is able to attract the lightning-bolt of illumination from on high.

But the Oak represents also a doorway – the word door itself originates from the Gaelic and Sanskrit *duir* – meaning solidity and protection as well as oak. This doorway is the entrance to the other realms. Much of Druid symbolism revolves around the concept of

Figure 5. A Moccas Park Oak – drawn by J. Strutt in 1830. Immortalised by the naturalist Francis Kilvert in the nineteenth century, Moccas Park in the Welsh borders is one of the finest examples of wood parkland in Britain. Kilvert's oaks – the 'grey old men of Moccas . . . [which] look as if they had been at the beginning and making of the world' are well over five hundred years old and are among the best specimens of this tree revered by the Druids

the entrance, gateway or door – to such an extent that the megalith builders went to enormous lengths to erect the massive stone doorways of the trilithons, as at Stonehenge, leading apparently nowhere. But the purpose of the doorway is always hidden from the uninitiated – the gateway between two trees or two stones will for one person be nothing but an empty space, but for the Druid will be the means whereby they can enter another state of consciousness, another realm of being. The secret 'oaken door' figures in the poems of Taliesin – and it is through this door that we encounter faerie beings and inner worlds of beauty and power. 'Knowledge of the oak', in other words being possessed of a Druid's knowledge, symbolises not only the ability to receive sudden illumination from above, but also the ability to enter the Otherworld through its doorway.

The oak symbolises strength, solidity, continuity of tradition, and endurance. Although not as long-lived as the yew, the oak often survives for over five hundred years, and frequently stood at the hub of a village as a symbol of its age and continuity. The oak was thus a tree that acted as a gathering-place for the populace – a remnant of the tradition that Druids taught under the oak tree. And it was Edward the Confessor who seemed to respond to this awareness of the oak as a sacred tree of meeting, by renewing the City of London's charter and swearing his oath upon the gospels at Gospel Oak in Highgate.

Oak forests once covered Britain and much of Europe – groves of oak trees would therefore have been numerous and the oak would have represented one of the most prominent and numerous of trees in ancient times. In folk tradition, the oak was sometimes personified as the Oak King, the god of the waxing year from the time of the winter solstice to the summer solstice. At midsummer he would do mock battle with the Holly King, who would then rule the waning year until the winter solstice, at which time the supremacy would revert once more to the Oak King. Midsummer fires were of oak, and midsummer is the time of the oak's flowering, and since it is also the central tree of Druid tradition, Robert Graves places it at the centre of the year, in the month running from 10 June to 7 July. Like the Roman god Janus, whom Graves associates with the Celtic god Llyr, the oak looks both ways at the centre-point of the year: back to the past of the year and forward to its future.

In Liz and Colin Murray's scheme, the oak is also the central month of the year – standing in the seventh of thirteen months. Given their beginning the year in November, however, the oak month falls in May, which seems to have less relevance than the midsummer month chosen by Graves. One connection with May, however, is that the oak was also the tree of the Celtic god Dagda, and it was the Dagda who supervised the boiling of a great cauldron of plenty, prototype of the grail – stirring it with a wooden spoon large enough to hold a man and woman coupled together. Here the Dagda, the spoon and the cauldron are seen as symbols of the fecundity of life – and it is at Beltane in May that the fundamental sexuality of nature becomes apparent in the flowering of the earth and in the coupling of both animals and humans.

The connection between this coupling and the mysteries of time and generation will become clearer when we examine a plant that has only sometimes been connected to the Ogham, but which has always been connected with Druidry – the mistletoe.

MISTLETOE

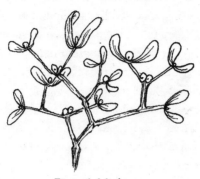

Figure 6. Mistletoe

The association of Druids with mistletoe is strong in the popular mind – and for good reason. Pliny, in his *Natural History*, spoke of the Druid custom of gathering mistletoe:

> The druids, for so call they their Magi, hold nothing more sacred than the mistletoe, and the tree on which it grows, provided it be the oak. They select a particular grove of oaks and perform no sacred rites without oak leaves, so that from this custom they may seem to have been called Druids (Oakites), according to the Greek interpretation of that word. They reckon whatever grows on these trees is sent down from Heaven and a proof that the tree itself is chosen by Deity. But the mistletoe is very rarely found and when found is sought after with the greatest religious ardour, and principally in the sixth moon, which is the beginning of their months and years, and when the tree is thirty years old it is then not half-grown only but has attained its full vigour. They call it All-Heal by a word in their own language . . .

The Druid's reverence for mistletoe comes from its symbolic association with male sperm owing to the colour and consistency of the mistleberry juice. Growing high up, the mistletoe has not touched the ground – it symbolises, therefore, seed-in-potency, in potential, awaiting the moment of conception. In ancient times, when the mistletoe was cut as described by Pliny and brought down from the tree, the Druid was undoubtedly enacting the process of incarnation, of fertilisation, of conception. The airborne seed symbolises the seed of the God which has not yet incarnated on earth – it is still on the world-tree – close to the heavens. The Druid cuts it down with a golden sickle – symbolising sun and moon, male and female power united. Conjunction – union – having occurred, the seed is brought to earth, the body of the Goddess, as it is brought down from the tree. In Druid ceremonies today we enact this at the time of the winter solstice – when the sun is reincarnated, or when the son is incarnated in the Christian tradition.

The mistletoe symbolises the moment of incarnation, the moment of entry-into-time. The oak symbolises the eternity of tradition. Oak and mistle united point to the mystery of the existence of both Time and No-Time, Form and No-Form. In the Druid ceremony of Alban Arthan, at the winter solstice, the mistletoe on the altar is, at the end, distributed to all present as a token and talisman for the times to come. We see an interesting survival of this custom until recent times in certain Christian churches: at York Cathedral a branch of mistle remained on the high altar for the twelve days of Christmas. In Wolverhampton and Staffordshire a similar tradition is recorded – the mistle being distributed afterwards to the congregation. And the connection between the mistle and fertilisation, or fertility, is with us still when we hang up the mistle-bunches at Christmas that will allow us to kiss beneath them.

CREATING NEW SACRED GROVES

Druid work with trees and plants is not simply ritualistic, symbolic or intellectual. Druids today believe strongly in the need to preserve and protect trees and to plant more of them. Druids get involved in campaigns to save ancient woodland or endangered species, and the Order of Bards, Ovates and Druids promotes a sacred grove planting programme that has initiated the planting of hundreds of new groves around the world. Details can be found on the Order's website and you can request a booklet from the Order about the programme, which gives information and help in planning and planting a grove.

To convey the Druid's belief about the value of trees and nature to us – both physical and spiritual – here is a statement that encapsulates the ideas shared by many, if not all, Druids today:

THE TREE OF DREAMS
'When one dreams alone it is only a dream.
When many dream together it is the beginning of a new reality.'
Hundertwasser

- Druids believe passionately in the need for each of us to love, cherish and protect the natural world.

- The health of our hearts, minds and bodies, of our children, and of our society depends upon the health of the natural world. If we pollute and damage the air, the rivers, the seas and the land, we pollute and damage ourselves, our children and our communities.

- Trees, plants, animals and stones are living spiritual beings, not simply physical objects. They have as much right to be here as we do.

- The tree offers an example of how we can be both powerful and peaceful. Though it is mighty it hurts no creature.

- The tree acts as a gateway to the Otherworld.

- It sows the seeds of our future on earth.

Destroy the forests and we destroy the dreams and the hopes of humanity.

 Each of us can become a force for good in the world – each of us can play a part in reversing the damage already caused. Just as the tree sows seeds for our future, so too can we sow seeds of hope and visions of beauty.

EXERCISE

'Approaching a tree we approach a sacred being who can teach us about love and about endless giving. They are one of millions of beings who provide our air, our homes, our fuel, our books. Working with the spirit of the tree can bring us renewed energy, powerful inspiration, deep communion.'

The quotation above is from the teaching material of the Ovate grade of the Order of Bards, Ovates and Druids. As an exercise in relation to this chapter, you might like to see if you can develop a relationship with a particular tree. See if you can sense how far its 'aura' or energy field extends. Experiment by walking towards and away from it, until you can feel the extent of its subtle influence. Ask the tree for permission to attune with it, and if you feel your request is accepted, spend time meditating beneath it, opening yourself to its inspiration.

CHAPTER ELEVEN

DRUID ANIMAL LORE

Look far off to the north-east
On the ocean so splendid
Teeming with life
Home of the seals
Shining and playful in the full tide
Ninth-century Irish verse

The joy of Druidry is that it helps us connect with life as it is now – not as it might have been thousands of years ago, or as it might be once we have died or gained enlightenment. It opens the door and says the mysteries are here – not in arcane books or hidden temples – but here in the world of nature that surrounds us. We have seen how this approach leads us out into the land – to feel the earth-currents, to walk the old tracks, to sit in the stone circles and gaze at the stars, to celebrate the passing of the seasons and the magic of the year, to touch the trees and learn their subtle wisdom. Now it is time for us to explore the part that animals play within Druidry.

Imagine that you are in a forest glade, a clearing lit by shafts of sunlight that filter down through the canopy of leaves high above. For a moment it seems as if you are alone in this clearing, but then you hear the sound of scuffling hooves, and all of a sudden you see a young hind approaching you – its graceful body caught in the sunbeams. She stops, and for a second the two of you simply stare at each other – each surprised, each entranced for a moment. Then she turns away from you, slowly and deliberately, and walks – not runs – back into the forest whence she came. She moves so slowly she seems to want you to follow her. You can almost hear her saying, 'Come with me. Follow me deeper into the forest.'

DEEPER INTO THE FOREST

Just as every plant and tree is considered sacred in Druidry, so every animal, fish and bird is seen as sacred too. But in the same way that some trees and plants, such as the oak and mistletoe, receive special veneration, so too do certain creatures receive particular attention within Druidry. The hind, which is a female red deer, is one such animal, and it is considered especially sacred by Druids. In Scotland they are called 'fairy cattle' and older people tell stories of seeing these creatures being milked on the mountaintops by fairies. Some say that the hinds are in fact fairy women themselves who have shape-shifted into this graceful form. To have a hind appear in our lives – either in the outer world or in the inner world in meditation or dreams – usually means that we will soon experience great happiness – that our lives are about to change in positive ways.

Each creature is seen in Druidry as offering gifts of inner knowledge, vitality and healing. We know that animals can provide us with food and clothing, but here the idea is that they can offer us much more – they are not simply 'dumb animals', fit only for our tables or shoes. Anyone who has kept, and truly loved, cats, dogs or horses, for example, will know of the extraordinary bonds that can form between we humans and the animals we love. Telepathic connections with pets are frequently reported, and have become the basis of scientific experiments, and it has now been proved that pet ownership in the elderly prolongs life and promotes good health. All this shows that animals do indeed offer us the gifts of vitality and healing, and clearly we in turn can help them with our care and affection.

In Druidry we go one stage further and suggest that each animal carries a different and very particular kind of 'energy' or healing potential – 'medicine' in Native American vocabulary. This energy is available to us not just through physically connecting with an animal. It simply isn't practical to stroke a snake or lion for example, but Druids believe they can still receive energy and interact with the animal in the Otherworld. This mysterious realm is sometimes called the Spiritworld. Some might think it imaginary, others might see it as another term for the Collective Unconscious, but Druids believe it is a world to which we sometimes travel in sleep or meditation, and which we enter at the death of our physical body. There, in this parallel universe of the Otherworld, are trees and plants, animals and birds, humans and nature-spirits. Just as our outer world contains a host of different environments and beings who inhabit them, so too with the Otherworld, and part of the training of Druidry lies in developing the ability to consciously travel in this world – so that in dreams and meditation, and on death, we can navigate within it.

Many of the old Celtic folk-tales that derive from the Druid tradition speak of this realm and of the exploits of mortals who enter it. In the story of the Well of Segais from Ireland, for example, we learn of King Cormac, who loses his wife and children to a mysterious warrior who spirits them away to the Otherworld. Cormac gives chase with an army, but a mist descends. He is separated from his troops, and he finds himself alone by a well. Around it grow nine hazel trees, and swimming in its deep waters are five large salmon who feed on the hazelnuts. Five streams representing the five senses flow from the well, which is also described as a fountain or pool. The mysterious warrior reappears and reveals himself as the god of the sea, Manannan, who reunites Cormac with his wife and children.

He then explains that the wise drink from each of the five streams and the central pool – suggesting an approach to wisdom that represents the very essence of Druidry as a sensuous spirituality that seeks wisdom and nourishment from the still centre of Spirit deep within *and* through each of our five senses.

The salmon is the creature that swims in the streams and the pool, and which represents the goal of every Druid – the Salmon of Wisdom. The salmon is perhaps the most sacred of all creatures in the Druid tradition, wherein it is known as the Oldest Animal. The fish as a central symbol within a spiritual tradition is ancient and ubiquitous – not only does it appear in Irish and Welsh legend, in the Vedas, in Hinduism and Buddhism, but also in Babylonian and Sumerian mythology. Orpheus was depicted as a fish, and so later were Christ and the Philosopher's Stone of the alchemists. Christian fish symbolism, including the custom of eating fish on a Friday, is believed to derive directly from the Jewish tradition, which in turn probably drew this element from Syrian belief. The fish and the fisherman were both intimately related symbolically from the earliest days – the first avatar of Vishnu the Creator was a fish, both the Buddha and Jesus are referred to as fishermen, the Babylonians had a fisher-god and the Fisher King is the central figure in the grail legend.

When the Druid today seeks the Salmon of Wisdom they are connecting not only to a tradition of the ancient Druids, but also to an understanding that is rooted deep in the collective awareness of all humanity.

WAYS OF WORKING WITH ANIMALS

A person moving through nature – however wild, remote,
even desolate the place may be – is never truly alone.
(Richard Nelson)

Since Druidry is a sensuous spirituality of the land that seeks an involvement with life, rather than a detachment from it, an essential way of working with animals from a Druid perspective is simply to include animals in our lives – spending time with them, caring for them, becoming involved in conservation projects. Western consumerism has tended to cut us off from much of life, enclosing us in boxes of metal as we shuttle from our brick boxes to our concrete and glass work-boxes. For many of us work involves gazing into the screen of a small box all day, to return home to an evening spent gazing at another box before falling asleep. Earth spiritualities such as Druidry offer a way out of these boxes built around us by our modern lifestyle. They encourage us to enter the natural world with an open heart and spirit to commune with the trees and the stones, the animals, the earth and the sky.

But in addition to simply being with and caring for animals more, Druidry also tells us that we can develop relationships with animals that go beyond the ordinary, and that animals in the Spiritworld as well as the physical world can guide and counsel, heal and protect us. They may come to us in our dreams, we may see them in our meditations, or we may encounter them in the outer world in magical and synchronistic ways.

Sometimes the animals that become meaningful for us are, in fact, symbolisations of parts of ourselves – the bull or horse might express aspects of our sexuality, the hawk or eagle our intellect, for example. A great deal of pioneering work has been done in this field by the psychologist Stephen Gallegos that demonstrates the psychotherapeutic value of working with our hidden fears, urges and wishes which can be evoked as animals that inhabit our inner world. But often the animals that we see in dreams or meditations or shamanic journeys are not simply symbolic representations, but are animals that exist as objective realities in the Otherworld as well as in the physical world. They may still evoke or resonate with our hidden fears or urges, but they exist independently of us, and are not just creations of our subconscious or our imagination. It is these magical animals that offer us special qualities, special 'medicines'.[56]

THE GIFTS OF THE ANIMALS

We discover the special qualities and gifts which these animals offer through experience – through exploring the world of animals and relating to them out in nature, and through interacting with them in the Otherworld too. The Ovate work in particular is focused on learning how to do this. But in addition to personal experience, we can also learn from the accumulated experience of our ancestors by studying traditional animal lore, and just as certain trees are associated in the Druid tradition with particular qualities, so certain animals have been found to mediate particular attributes too. For example: the bear, boar, cat, dog, goose, otter and raven are all associated with the quality of protection; the adder, boar, dog, frog, ram and raven are connected with healing; the owl and raven with initiation, and so on. When we need the qualities or abilities that these animals represent, we can call upon them to help us – seeing and relating to them in our inner world, dancing or singing with them, and connecting with them in the outer world too.

RAVEN KNOWLEDGE

In the old stories Druids were sometimes referred to as 'adders' – those with 'serpent knowledge' – and sometimes they were described as those with 'raven knowledge'. As the associations listed above show, the raven possesses many attributes – mediating healing, prophetic knowledge, protection, and initiatory power.

The raven is seen as a messenger between the two worlds – this and the next – and for this reason we find ravens buried at the bottom of ancient ritual pits, such as at Danebury in Hampshire. These pits or shafts symbolised the connection between this world and the Otherworld, and the raven was seen as a messenger between the two.

The early Irish Druids divined according to the flight and cries of birds, and in particular the raven, and the idea of the raven as a bird of divination and prophecy was lodged so firmly in the folk imagination that as late as 1694 in Hertfordshire a raven was reported to have uttered a prophecy three times. Even today the association of the raven with prophecy and protection is openly fostered in the heart of London at the Tower. In the tale of Bran the Blessed, the prophetic god-king Bran (which means 'raven') asks that his head be cut off and buried on the White Mount in London, facing the direction of France. As long as his head remained buried there it would protect the kingdom. The Tower of London was later built on the site of the White Mount, and the magical protective power of the buried head was symbolised by the presence of ravens, which are kept at the Tower to the present day to fulfil Bran's prophecy and ensure the safety of the realm.

ANIMAL ORACLES, ALLIES AND FAMILIARS

Today we can work with the sacred animals of tradition to gain guidance and insight into our lives, and a number of animal oracles have been developed to help us do this – including *The Beasts of Albion* and *The Druid Animal Oracle*.

Sometimes we seem to have a special connection with one or more animals – we feel an affinity with them, they come to us in our dreams, we turn to them in our minds and hearts when we need strength or reassurance. By working with specific techniques to strengthen our bonds with them, these animals can become our spiritual companions, and as our relationship with them deepens, we may feel that they have become our 'familiars' – our totem animals – who stay close to us and become our magical allies, partners in our journey through life.

The animals themselves then teach us, and we can draw as well on the fund of animal lore embodied in tradition – in the old stories and sayings that simply need some thought and time to unlock their secrets, as we can see from the old English adage: *Ask the wild bee what the Druids knew.*

EXERCISE

After reading this chapter, spend a few moments forgetting all that you have read. Make yourself comfortable and allow yourself to come to a sense of inner centredness and calm. Close your eyes and feel all your concerns falling away from you. Focus for a while on your breathing, and then slowly imagine that you are walking through the forest towards a clearing. As you approach this clearing in the woods you notice that it feels unusually peaceful and calm. There is a special atmosphere here. You find a tree on the edge of the clearing that feels just right for you and you lean against its trunk, and look up at its crown towering high above you. Then you look around this glade, breathing in the smell of the earth, the trees and the flowers, and enjoying the sunlight as it filters down through the trees to the forest floor.

Think about the realm of the animals and ask if you can meet an animal or bird that can bring you just the kind of energy, healing or guidance that you need. Without thinking rationally about this, just allow the animal or bird to appear in the clearing of its own accord, and enjoy its company, and be sensitive to the qualities it brings you and any message it might have.

When you are ready to finish, thank the animal for its gift, then see it leave the clearing, and gradually allow your awareness of the glade and the forest surrounding it to dissolve as you become aware of being in your everyday consciousness again, here and now, refreshed and revitalised.

CHAPTER TWELVE

DRUIDRY, WICCA AND THE CRAFT OF MAGIC

*I fancy that certain practices, such as the use of the
circle to keep the power in, were local inventions,
derived from the use of the Druid or pre-Druid circle.*
Gerald Gardner, *Witchcraft Today*

Druidry and Wicca represent the two main streams of indigenous 'earth spirituality' of western European culture. But
though their roots are buried deep in the foundations of that culture,
the ways in which they are practised today were formulated only
recently and, as we shall see, there are many connections between
the two approaches.

In the 1930s or 40s two men met and became friends and co-
workers, probably first at the idyllic naturist community of

Spielplatz in Hertfordshire. One was a Druid, the other a poet and historian. Gerald Gardner, a member of the Ancient Druid Order and the Folklore Society, met the poet and teacher Ross Nichols, and discovered that he shared his interest in magic, the occult and the pre-Christian past of Britain. After more than a decade of friendship, Ross became a Druid too, joining the Ancient Order in 1954. This was the same year that Gardner's first work of non-fiction on witchcraft was published – *Witchcraft Today*. This book heralded the popularisation of Wicca and began the process that led to it becoming such a significant and dynamic spirituality today.

At about the time the book was published, Ross took my father to meet Gerald Gardner at their naturist club. They lay in the sun, talked about history and swam in the pool. My father, as editor of a history magazine, would later commission Ross to write articles, but at this time it was Ross who was the editor. He had just finished editing an English translation of Paul Christian's massive *History and Practice of Magic* and had gone on to edit Gardner's book – quite a task according to writers Francis King and Doreen Valiente, since Gardner was not a skilled author.

Already, before the book was published, Gardner had established a coven, and was hoping to start a Druid group on the Isle of Man. As far as we know Ross did not join his coven, and although interested in Wicca, never considered himself a witch. Instead he continued to pursue his interests in mythology and the seasonal festivals, and began to develop a passion for Druidry. In the end, when Gardner and the old Druid Chief died in 1964, Ross introduced a new kind of Druid practice into the world. It was based on the old lore – on the mythology of Britain and Ireland, on the old bardic tales, on the practices of the Ancient Druid Order, and on ideas drawn from folklore, depth psychology and legend. But it was new because it took all of this material and presented it through the structure of a mystery school that, like Wicca, drew much of its practical inspiration from the immense heritage of the Western magical tradition, which – in a perfect arc – connected the Pythagorean and neo-Pythagorean roots of Western magic to the Pythagoreanism of the ancient Druids. Just like Wicca, this Druidry worked with the magic circle blessed by fire and water, and with the four natural elements together with a fifth – Spirit – symbolised by the Pythagorean pentagram. It offered three grades or degrees, entered by initiation, of Bard, Ovate and Druid, as opposed to Wicca's first, second and third degrees. And it celebrated the same eight seasonal festivals.

Gardner, in a later book, *The Meaning of Witchcraft*, speculated that the ancient Druids represented the scholarly élite while witch-craft was the religion of the peasants, and whether or not this is true, this perception has affected our views of the two paths. Druidry often appears to be the more scholarly or learned path, while Wicca appears to be the more earthy, intuitive or instinctual way. The two founding fathers of these types of practice certainly embodied these differences – Ross tended to be the dry academic, Gardner the earthy maverick. But things have come a long way since they presented their systems to the world – scholarly approaches in Wicca and instinctual and intuitive approaches in Druidry have developed in tandem, and now many people creatively blend Wiccan and Druidic approaches and find them complementary.

FOUNDING MOTHERS

Although Gardner and Nichols were undoubtedly seminal in their influence on these two strands of modern spirituality, we must remember that new movements that capture the public imagination and grow in popularity do not arise in a vacuum. Both men were influenced by the spirit of the times, whose agenda in post-war Britain urgently required a return to a peaceful harmony with the land. They were both driven by the need in the collective soul for spiritualities that honoured and celebrated the earth and all life, rather than for religions that urged us to transcend nature and the body. And they were influenced, too, by other people – particularly by two women, Doreen Valiente and Vera Chapman, who, if we are to term Gardner and Nichols founding fathers, we should term founding mothers of the movements they initiated.

Gardner met Valiente in 1952 and immediately encouraged her to improve and augment the rituals in the Wiccan Book of Shadows – a term for the book used to record Wiccan rites, which Gardner apparently adopted on reading of its use in India in an article published in *The Occult Observer* by a friend of Ross. Valiente, who knew Ross too, wrote inspired poetry with an unashamed expression of sensuality and paganism. Vera Chapman, who matched Ross in both her depth of learning and her fascination for history and poetry, was a successful author, keen proponent of women's Freemasonry, a member of the Woodcraft-related Kibbo Kift movement and the founder of the Tolkien Society. Like Ross she was also interested in a fairer distribution of wealth, and supported the Social Credit movement. Ross appointed her Pendragon of his Order, and after the success of her Arthurian trilogy, Warner Bros. bought the film rights, using her work as the basis for a disappointing cartoon film – *Quest for Camelot*.

Since Valiente and Chapman, other women have contributed immensely to both traditions – bringing a depth and warmth to these spiritualities that now appeal to women just as much as to men. Leaders of Druid groups today tend to have a grounding in Wicca as well as Druidry, and many Wiccans also study Druidry. Each system is complete in itself and some people choose to practise just one, or to practise both at different times. Others choose to combine elements of both ways, and I have explored how this can be done in *Druidcraft – the Magic of Wicca and Druidry*.

There are many varieties of Wicca now, just as there are many different styles of Druid practice, which makes it hard to offer comparisons, but on the whole Wicca tends to offer a more defined theology, often calling itself a religion, with most Wiccans believing that Deity exists in the form of the Goddess and her consort, the God. Contemporary Druidry, as we have seen, is considerably less precise, leaving it up to each Druid to decide on his or her conception of Deity. As a result, although much Druid and Wiccan ceremonial is similar, their focus and atmosphere can be quite different. While Wicca tends to work with the Goddess and the God, and with the power of the union of the opposites, Druidry tends to work with the results of this union in creativity, and deals not so much with the gods as with the fruit of their inspiration in poetry and story. Both ways of working are powerful and valid in their own right and need no additions, but they also work well together.[57]

Many Druids share the same conception of Deity with Wiccans, but leaving aside theological considerations, solitary practitioners of Wicca, often calling themselves 'Hedge Witches' are practically indistinguishable from solitary Ovates, or 'Hedge Druids'. They share the same interests in attuning themselves to the powers of nature, and in healing, herbalism, and divination.

A common misunderstanding associates Druids with male sun-worshippers and Wiccans with female moon-worshippers. In reality both Druidry and Wicca reverence earth, sun, moon and stars equally, and nowadays Wiccan and Druid groups tend to have equal numbers of both sexes. Whereas a while ago Wiccan and Druid groups were structured differently – with covens being small and private and groves often being larger and more public – the situation has changed considerably in recent years. This has largely come about as a result of the cross-fertilisation between the two movements, and the Wiccan author Vivianne Crowley speaks of this recent development when she says:

> ... Much has changed. Druidry has developed greater interest in the traditional magical skills and gifts of its Druid ancestors, and the role of women in Druidry now equals that of men. Wicca has grown closer to Druidry in its provision for family participation and openness as a path for the many rather than the few. Both traditions have evolved to see themselves as part of a growing contemporary spirituality that is concerned with social engagement, planetary responsibility, and providing meaningful philosophy and ethics by which people may live in our increasingly complex multi-cultural world.[58]

SPELLCRAFT AND THE MAGICS OF MAKING, QUESTING AND CHANGING

At the beginning of this book I mentioned that Druidry offers at least seven gifts to the world – one of which is the gift of magic. Books on Wicca tend to discuss magic quite openly, and spellcraft is often taught from the beginning of Wiccan training. But even though Druidry is fundamentally a magical spirituality, books on Druidry usually avoid the subject of magic, and spellcraft is hardly ever mentioned. This is because the topic of magic can so easily generate 'glamour', and far from leading us closer to wisdom, can ensnare us in delusion.

The problem with the kind of magic that involves the casting of spells, aside from the danger of the misuse of power from insuffi- cient psychological and ethical development, is that it is so easy for an interest in this activity to feed an attitude of consumerism that tempts people to fall yet again into the trap of believing that happi- ness or fulfilment will come from getting things or having things. The type of magical experience that Druidry fosters is quite the reverse – it is the type of experience you get when you trek out into the wilds of nature and you are overwhelmed with a feeling of awe that has nothing to do with owning or getting anything. When you can look at life, and experience that none of it belongs to you, quite magically and paradoxically you can feel then – in the depths of your being – that you truly belong in the world.

So the magic taught and practised within Druidry, at least in the Order of Bards, Ovates and Druids, concerns not the attempt to manipulate circumstances or to 'get things', but instead the art of opening to the magic of being alive, the art of bringing ideas into manifestation, and the art of journeying in quest of healing, inspira- tion and knowledge.

These kinds of magic taught within the Order fall into three categories: the Magic of Making, the Magic of Questing, and the Magic of Changing.

The Magic of Making concerns the process whereby something as subtle and intangible as a thought, an inspiration, an idea, can be encouraged to manifest in the world. It is the magic of the creative process, and the province of the Bard. The work of attuning to the natural world and the world of Spirit helps us to receive Awen – inspiration. An understanding of the two different sides of ourselves, masculine and feminine, helps us to grow and parent the child of that inspiration, and the whole emphasis of the bardic training on the expression of our creativity encourages its nurturing and manifestation.

The Magic of Questing involves journeying, either in the Otherworld or in this world, to search for inspiration or knowledge, healing or insight. This is the province of the Ovate, who may undertake a magical journey in the physical world to seek auguries and new understanding, through a pilgrimage or vision quest; or who may undertake a journey in the Otherworld through a sweat-house ceremony, meditation, guided visualisation or shamanic journey.

The Magic of Changing is the magic of transformation – the alchemical process that leads us towards a greater sense of wholeness, integration and empowerment. Once we understand that the most effective way to change our outer lives is to change our inner lives, then the types of spells that we might craft are altogether different from those which seek to manipulate circumstances or obtain material benefits. Although this is the province of the Druid, the work of every grade is fundamentally alchemical and facilitates transformation.

The attitude of Druidry is that life itself is magical, and that our journey through life is a magical one. Our task is to unburden our hearts and minds and to free our souls so that we can experience that magic and in our turn contribute more of it to the world. To do this, as Marcel Proust realised, involves an inner transformation: 'The real magic,' he said, 'lies not in seeking new landscapes but in having new eyes.'

EXERCISE

Imagine you are about to study magic. Which magic would you like to learn, and why?

CHAPTER THIRTEEN

THE HEART
OF THE
MYSTERY

Turning around and around in a circle,
Spiralling towards the centre,
We know that we have come to the centre of who we are.
We crouch on the earth, we touch her with our hands.
We know that we have come to be with her.
Finding ourselves we have found our connection with nature.
We sing, we speak poetry, we chant, we make music
– finding our hearts we have found the heart of the mystery.
Finding the depths we have found the Way to be simple.

D ruidry is not a complicated path. Appreciating it involves reorienting oneself so that one can approach the mysterious, the feminine, the arts, both aesthetic and esoteric, in a way that allows us to let go of our assumptions and presumptions about life and instead carries us, as in a Druid ceremony, around the circle of our life towards the still point at the centre of which is both our true self and the divine source.

The call to this way is being heard again – throughout the world – because it represents not an eccentric, irrelevant and atavistic belief system, but an approach to life that can unite the spiritual and the artistic, the environmental and the humanitarian concerns we share, the thirst for connection with Mother Earth and with Father Sun – the need for a powerful but natural spirituality, and the need for a down-to-earth, sensual, fully human connection with our bodies and the body of our home, the earth.

One of the most moving moments that can occur on our spiritual and psychological journey is the discovery of the inner child that exists within us – whatever our age. However careful our upbringing might have been, it seems inevitable that we first experience this inner child as hurt and rejected. Once, however, we open ourselves to it, no longer pretending or living as if it didn't exist, we find that this child within is in fact a divine child, a radiant seed-being of God/dess. Within a Christian framework we can say that we experience the reality and the presence of the Christ-child within our hearts. The Druid tradition speaks of the same mystery, but calls the child the Mabon.

In a peculiar reflection of the story of the prodigal son, it is we as adults who turn to the child to recognise him or her as the manifestation of divinity within us. And it is we as adults who come to understand that much of the negativity that we experienced and expressed came from the desperation of the wounded child who needed to be acknowledged and heard. In our struggle to 'grow up' we ignored the voice that became buried deeper and deeper in our hearts.

A similar process of burial has occurred on a collective level. It is said that beneath the cathedrals of Saint Paul's in London and Notre Dame in Paris lie stone circles, forgotten by a culture which has denied its roots. The consequences of this denial have made us act in a way that Thomas Berry suggests is like that of the autistic child – the child who cannot face the world, and who seems not to see or hear even though we know they can. They are emotionally isolated from their fellow creatures but are fascinated by mechanical devices. We, as a culture, are obsessed with mechanics – we no longer hear the voice of the river or the sea, we can no longer let the 'outer world flow into our beings'.[59]

Unconsciously or consciously we have despised our origins because we believed our ancestors were savage brutish beings. In the same way we unconsciously despise the child who lives in our hearts as a weak and ignorant creature. But the stone which has been rejected shall be the cornerstone of the temple: when we turn to the child and see it for who it really is, it offers us the potential to transform our lives, and when we turn to our past and see it for all that it really represents, it in turn has the potential to transform our future – to give birth to the dream in our hearts.

Seen in this way, Druidry can be considered as cultural therapy – a way of collective healing and regeneration. We have seen how the Druidic roots of our culture can be viewed in either of two ways. Our ancestors can be seen as barbarian, primitive and ignorant, living in a world 'nasty, brutish and short', or they can be seen as wise, noble philosophers and mystics, versed in mathematics, engineering, and astronomical skills.

In the first view of Druidry, we espouse the theory of original stupidity, which sees humanity struggling from the darkness of prehistoric ignorance to the light of present-day scientific knowledge. The second view recognises that our foundations grew out of an age of light rather than darkness.

The way we view our origins determines the way we relate to the world. Pelagius was a fourth-century British theologian who challenged the concept of original sin. Some say he was a Druid. We cannot be sure whether he was or not, but he was certainly deeply influenced by their heritage. He taught the doctrine of original blessing, insisting that a baby is born blessed and innocent rather than sinful. He was persecuted by the Church and chased out of Europe, dying in either Africa or the Middle East, though some say he might have found refuge in his last years in a monastery in Wales.[60]

Perhaps Pelagius knew that if we believe we are rooted in primitive ignorance and original sin, then however hard we try, we will unconsciously act in ignorant and destructive ways. But the reverse also applies, and the time has come now for the return of the forgotten, the denied and the repressed. The time has come for us to acknowledge fully that our origins – our source and our basis – are divine.

Our roots are holy.

RESOURCES AND RECOMMENDED READING

But we shall never understand Druidism unless we grasp the fact that it was recognised that all knowledge must be sought in two directions: one, by searching the outer world – Science; and two, by searching the depths of the human soul and the secrets of the human body – Art.

Eleanor Merry, *The Flaming Door*

THE INTERNET

The internet is a powerful resource for anyone wishing to learn more about Druidry. Just type 'Druidry' or 'Druid' into a search engine and a wealth of sites will be offered to you. As always with websites discrimination is needed – there are many wonderful sites, but also ones that may not be worth viewing. The Order of Bards, Ovates and Druids website at http://druidry.org has over a thousand pages of information that includes a library, a guided journey and meditation, sections on Druid camps, the Sacred Grove Planting Programme, the Campaign for Ecological Responsibility, training in Druidry, a bookshop, and comprehensive links to many other sites.

COURSES AND GROUPS

The Order of Bards, Ovates and Druids runs an experience-based home-learning course that guides you through the three grades of Bard, Ovate and Druid. Each month teaching material is mailed to you, and you have the support of a mentor with whom you can correspond by letter or email. In addition there are workshops, camps and celebrations in Britain and the USA and other parts of the world, and over fifty groves and seed-groups where you can meet and work with other members. The course is also available in French, German and Dutch. Full details from: OBOD, PO Box 1333, Lewes, East Sussex, BN7 1DX. Tel/fax (+44) (0)1273 419129 Email office@druidry.org or see http://druidry.org

There are currently no other distance-learning courses of this kind available, but Druidry today is a vibrant and growing move-ment and there are many groups who offer training and support in other ways, through meetings, workshops, ceremonies, magazines, and camps. To obtain information on these, the best resource is Philip Shallcrass and Emma Restall Orr's book *A Druid Directory*, published by the British Druid Order.

The British Druid Order runs camps and workshops, organises festivals and celebrations and publishes books and two magazines. They can be contacted at BDO, PO Box 1217, Devizes, Wiltshire SN10 4XA or via http://www.druidorder.demon.co.uk. Their *Druid Directory* offers a comprehensive guide to most of the many Druid groups in Britain, and some abroad. Each group describes itself and gives contact details, and in addition the book provides an excellent concise history and overview of the subject. Copies are available from the BDO and from the OBOD bookshop.

In the USA the two main Druid groups are *Keltria*, PO Box 48369 Minneapolis MN 55448-0369, http://www.keltria.org and *ADF*, 859 N. Hollywood Way, Box 368, Burbank, CA 91505, http://www.adf.org.

BOOKS

To introduce the subject to someone who is new to this field, a simple and inspiring brief guide to Druidry accompanied by beautiful photographs of nature is *Druidry*, by Emma Restall Orr (Thorsons 2001).

For introductory books on the Druid path see *The Principles of Druidry*, by Emma Restall Orr (Thorsons, 1998), *Druids – A Beginner's Guide*, by Cairistiona Worthington (Hodder, 1999) and *A Guide to Druidry*, by Philip Shallcrass (Piatkus, 2000). Each book is short and easy to read, and includes practical exercises. Although these are introductory volumes, their authors have years of experience in Druidry, and each book contributes something unique to an understanding of what Druidism is, and how it can help you.

You might like to supplement your study of these primers by treating yourself to one or more of the larger illustrated books on the Druids. These include *Exploring the World of the Druids*, by Dr Miranda Aldhouse Green (Thames & Hudson, 1998), which is filled with excellent illustrations and photographs and gives a wonderfully broad introduction to the history of Druidism, both ancient and modern, and *Celtic Bards, Celtic Druids*, by R. J. Stewart and Robin Williamson (Blandford, 1996), in which essays by these two well-known authors alternate with renditions of some of the key old tales and stunning colour illustrations.

For a history of ancient Druidry see *The Druids*, by Peter Beresford Ellis (Constable, 1995) and *The Druids – Celtic Priests of Nature*, by Jean Markale (Inner Traditions, 1999).

For an inspirational book to act as your companion through the year, consider the following: *Celtic Devotional – Daily Prayers and Blessings*, by Caitlin Matthews (Godsfield, 1996) – prayers, poems, exercises, rituals and suggestions by a great Celtic scholar and past Presider of the Order of Bards, Ovates and Druids; *The Celtic Spirit – Daily Meditations for the Turning Year*, by Caitlin Matthews (HarperSanFrancisco, 1999) – quotations, questions, essays and meditations for each day of the year; and *Kindling the Celtic Spirit*, by Mara Freeman (HarperSanFrancisco, 2001) – An Honorary Bard of

OBOD offers teachings, poetry, recipes, stories and folklore related to each of the seasons; *Anam Cara – A Book of Celtic Wisdom*, by John O'Donoghue (HarperCollins, 1997) – essays which inspire and enchant with their unique use of language.

Much Druid wisdom is contained within the old stories. There are many editions of the old Celtic tales, but these are especially recommended: *Druids, Gods and Heroes from Celtic Mythology*, by Anne Ross (Peter Lowe, 1986); *Celtic Myths, Celtic Legends*, by R. J. Stewart (Blandford, 1996); *An Introduction to Celtic Mythology*, by David Bellingham (Grange Books, 1996); and *The Mabinogion* and *Early Irish Myths and Sagas*, both translated by Jeffrey Gantz (Penguin, 1976).

To explore aspects of Druidry in depth see: *The Bardic Source Book*, edited by John Matthews (Blandford, 1998); *The Celtic Seer's Source Book*, edited by John Matthews (Blandford, 2000); *The Druid Source Book*, edited by John Matthews (Blandford, 1996); *The Encyclopaedia of Celtic Wisdom*, edited by John and Caitlin Matthews (Rider, 2001); and *The Making of a Druid: Hidden Teachings from the Colloquy of Two Sages*, by Christian J. Guyonvarc'h (Inner Traditions, 2002).

To explore the work of Ross Nichols, a biography, photographs and selections of his paintings and poetry can be found at http://druidry.org. See also *The Book of Druidry*, by Ross Nichols (Thorsons, 1990); *In the Grove of the Druids – the Druid Teachings of Ross Nichols*, by Philip Carr-Gomm (Watkins, 2002); and *Prophet, Priest and King – the Poetry of Philip Ross Nichols*, edited and introduced by Jay Ramsay (Oak Tree Press, 2001).

To explore the shamanic aspects of Druidry see *Fire in the Head – Shamanism and the Celtic Spirit*, by Tom Cowan (HarperSanFrancisco, 1993).

To explore the relationship between Druidry and Wicca see *Druidcraft – the Magic of Wicca and Druidry*, by Philip Carr-Gomm (Thorsons, 2002).

To see how a Druidic understanding can be used when exploring the landscape see *The Druid Way*, by Philip Carr-Gomm (Element Books, 1993).

For a wide range of contributions from Druids around the world, which include essays on history, healing, ritual, herbs, star lore and more, see *The Druid Renaissance*, edited by Philip Carr-Gomm (Thorsons, 1996).

DIVINATION SYSTEMS

The following sets can provide important insights and experiences based upon Druid tree and animal lore: *The Celtic Tree Oracle*, by Liz and Colin Murray (Rider, 1989) – a set of cards and a book which works with the sacred trees of the Celts and Druids and the Ogham; *Celtic Wisdom Sticks*, by Caitlin Matthews – a bag of Ogham staves and a book which explains their oracular use (Connections, 2001); *The Druid Animal Oracle*, by Philip and Stephanie Carr-Gomm (Fireside Books, 1995 (USA); Connections, 1996 (UK)) – a set of cards and a book which works with the sacred animals of the Celtic and Druid traditions (also available in French, German, Italian, and Dutch editions); and *The Beasts of Albion*, by Miranda Gray (Thorsons, 1995) – a set of cards and a book which works with sacred animals of Britain.

GLOSSARY

Alban Arthan – poetically translated as 'The Light of Arthur', the Druid festival of the winter solstice.

Alban Eilir – poetically translated as 'The Light of the Earth', the Druid festival of the spring equinox.

Alban Elfed – poetically translated as 'The Light of Water', the Druid festival of the autumn equinox.

Alban Hefin – poetically translated as 'The Light of the Shore', the Druid festival of the summer solstice.

Awen – inspiration, the gift or blessing of the gods generally, or the goddess Ceridwen, Patroness of the Bards, specifically.

Bard – in ancient times, a poet and story-teller who trained in a bardic college. In modern times, one who sees their creativity as an innate spiritual ability, and who chooses to nurture that ability partly or wholly with Druidism.

Beltane/Bealteinne – the Druid festival dedicated to celebrating spring and the union of god and goddess. Meaning 'The Good Fire', Beltane celebrations usually include leaping over a bonfire. Celebrated around 1 May in the northern hemisphere, 1 October in the southern.

Druid – in ancient times a philosopher, teacher, counsellor and magician, the word probably meaning 'A Forest Sage' or 'Strong Seer'. In modern times, one who follows Druidry as their chosen spiritual path, or who has entered the Druid level of training in a Druid order.

Druidcraft – a type of spiritual practice that combines Druidry with the 'craft' of Wicca.

Eisteddfod – a bardic festival and competition of the performing arts, from the Welsh. Usually opened with a Druid ceremony.

Equinox – the times in spring and autumn when day and night are of equal duration. They represent times of balance and also turning points of the year as the seasons change, and are celebrated in Druidry with ceremonies.

Imbolc/Oimelc – the Druid festival of the goddess, particularly Brighid, celebrated around 1 February in the northern hemisphere, 1 August in the southern.

Inner world – Our personal inner world that exists in our imagination or psyche that can sometimes connect us to an objective, transpersonal Otherworld.

Lughnasadh/Lammas – the Druid festival of the harvest, celebrated around 1 August in the northern hemisphere, 1 February in the southern.

Nwyfre – the Druid term for 'life-force', probably derived from an ancient Celtic word *naomh* – firmament.

Otherworld – The world or reality that exists in parallel with the physical/everyday world which we visit sometimes in dreams or meditation and to where Druids believe we travel on the death of the physical body. Used synonymously with the term 'Spiritworld'.

Ovate – in ancient times a prophet, seer, healer and diviner. In modern times, one who studies or practises herbalism, healing and divination within a Druidic context, or who has entered the Ovate level of training within a Druid order.

Pheryllt – Druid alchemists, said to have lived in Snowdonia, Wales.

Samhuinn/Samhain – the Druid festival of the ancestors – a time for honouring those who have died, celebrated around 1 November in the northern hemisphere, 1 May in the southern.

Solstice – the time in summer when the day is longest, and in winter when the day is shortest. Solstices are times of powerful celestial and terrestrial influence, and are celebrated in Druidry with ceremonies.

Spiritworld – *see* Otherworld.

Summerlands/The Blessed Isles/Hy Breasil – terms used in Druidry for the realm that exists in the Otherworld that we travel to on the death of the physical body.

NOTES

1. Speech to the North American Conference on Religion and Ecology, Washington 18 May 1990.

2. See, for example, Graham Hancock, *Fingerprints of the Gods*, Crown, 1996.

3. A system of spiritual development based on Steiner's clairvoyant insights, which seeks to optimise physical and mental health and wellbeing.

4. Eleanor C. Merry, *The Flaming Door – The Mission of the Celtic Folk-Soul*, Floris Books, 1983.

5. Christine Hartley, *The Western Mystery Tradition*, Aquarian Press, 1968.

6. Caitlin Matthews, *The Elements of the Celtic Tradition*, Element Books, 1989.

7. All classical quotations given in this book can be found in John Matthews (ed.), *The Druid Source Book*, Blandford, 1996.

8. Kenneth Jackson, *The Oldest Irish Tradition: a Window on the Iron Age*, Cambridge University Press, 1964.

9. Alexander Carmichael (ed.), *Carmina Gadelica*, Scottish Academic Press, 1972.

10. See Stuart Piggott, *The Druids*, Thames & Hudson, 1985.

11. Jean-Pierre Mohen, *The World of Megaliths*, Cassell, 1989.

12. Colin Renfrew, *Archaeology and Language – the Puzzle of Indo-European Origins*, Penguin, 1989.

13. Sylvain Levi, quoted in M. Dillon, 'The Archaism of Irish Tradition', *Proceedings of the British Academy*, 33 (1947). For a comprehensive survey of the similarities and connections between Indian and Celtic traditions, see Alwyn Rees and Brinley Rees, *Celtic Heritage*, Thames & Hudson, 1989.

14. Cited in Philip Carr-Gomm, *Druidcraft – the Magic of Wicca and Druidry*, Thorsons, 2002.

15. See Peter Beresford Ellis, *The Druids*, Constable, 1995.

16. Piggott, *The Druids*.

17. See the Patrician Texts in the *Book of Armagh*, L. Bieler, 1979. Quoted in C. Oakley, 'Druids and Witches', in P. Carr-Gomm (ed.), *The Druid Renaissance*, Thorsons, 1996.

18. Merry, *The Flaming Door*.

19. See T. Freke and P. Gandy, *The Jesus Mysteries*, Thorsons, 1999.

20. Robert Graves, *The White Goddess*, Faber & Faber, 1961.

21. From *The Penitential of Burchard of Worms*.

22. Quotations on this page are cited in Piggott, *The Druids*, Chapter 4.

23. An illustration of the 'Archdruidess of Kew' can be found in R. Nichols, *The Book of Druidry*, Thorsons, 1990.

24. For the official website of the Royal National Eisteddfod of Wales, see: http://www.eisteddfod.org.uk

25. J. M. Greer, *Awen – A Book of Druid Lore*, in preparation.

26. Jay Ramsay (ed. and intro.), *Prophet, Priest and King – The Poetry of Philip Ross Nichols*, The Oak Tree Press, 2001.

27. A section on the relationship between naturism and Druidry, including articles, quotations and archive photographs, can be seen at http://druidry.org

28. Republished as John Michell, *The New View Over Atlantis*, Thames & Hudson, 1983.

29. John Lilly, *The Centre of the Cyclone*, Paladin, 1973.

30. Michael Harner, *The Way of the Shaman*, Harper & Row, 1980.

31. See John Purser, *Scotland's Music*, Mainstream Publishing, 1992. Recordings of prehistoric instruments can be heard on *The Kilmartin*

CD, copies of which are available from the OBOD Bookshop at
http://druidry.org

32. See Beresford Ellis, *The Druids*, p.176.

33. R. J. Stewart, *The Prophetic Vision of Merlin*, Arkana, 1986.

34. See A. Allen, *A Dictionary of Sussex Folk Medicine*, Countryside
Books, 1995.

35. For more information on Nwyfre, see Carr-Gomm, *Druidcraft –
the Magic of Wicca and Druidry*.

36. For a comparison of Maori and Brehon laws, see Jim Consedine,
Restorative Justice, Plough Shed Publications (New Zealand), 1999.

37. A web search under 'Brehon laws' will reveal a number of good
summaries.

38. Matthews, *Elements of the Celtic Tradition*.

39. E. Hull, *The Folklore of the British Isles*, n.p., 1928, pp 272–3.

40. The complete text of this ritual is given in Nichols, *The Book of
Druidry*.

41. See Carr-Gomm, *Druidcraft – the Magic of Wicca and Druidry*.

42. See R. Hutton, *Stations of the Sun – The History of the Ritual Year
in Britain*, Oxford University Press, 1996.

43. Examples of naming, wedding and funeral rites can be found in
Philip Carr-Gomm, *The Druid Way*, Element Books, 1993. See also
E. Restall Orr, *Ritual*, Thorsons, 2000.

44. Translated by Caitlin Matthews in Matthews, *Elements of the
Celtic Tradition*.

45. See Tom Graves, *Needles of Stone Revisited*, Gothic Image, 1986.

46. The results of this research are summarised in Paul Devereux,
Places of Power, Blandford, 1990, and *Earthlights Revelation*,
Blandford, 1989.

47. See D. Robbins, 'The Dragon Project and the Talking Stones',
New Scientist, 21 October 1982.

48. Alexander Thom, *Megalithic Sites in Britain*, Oxford University
Press, 1967.

49. See H. Paterson, *The Celtic Lunar Zodiac*, Rider, 1992, and *The
Handbook of Celtic Astrology : The 13-Sign Lunar Zodiac of the Ancient
Druids*, Llewellyn, 1994.

50. See K. Critchlow, *Time Stands Still*, Gordon Fraser, 1979.

51. See Paul Devereux, *Stone Age Soundtracks, The Acoustic Archaeology of Ancient Sites*, Vega, 2002.

52. This is a quotation from Carr-Gomm, *The Druid Way*. For a guide to contemporary stone circle building see R. L. Roy, *Stone Circles – A Modern Builders Guide to the Megalithic Revival*, Chelsea Green, 1999.

53. See Richard St Barbe Baker, *My Life, My Trees*, Ecology, 1985.

54. See Caitlin and John Matthews, *The Encyclopaedia of Celtic Wisdom*, Rider, 2001, Chapter 2; K. Ogham Naddair, *Koelbren and Runic* (2 vols), Edinburgh, Keltia Publications, 1986–7; S. Ogam O'Boyle, *The Poet's Secret*, Gilbert Dalton, 1980; Graves, *The White Goddess*.

55. See J. M. Paterson, *Tree Wisdom*, Thorsons, 1996.

56. See Eligio Stephen Gallegos, *Personal Totem Pole: Animal Imagery, The Chakras and Psychotherapy*, Moon Bear Press, 1990.

57. For an exploration of this subject, see Carr-Gomm, *Druidcraft – the Magic of Wicca and Druidry*.

58. Ibid., Preface.

59. Thomas Berry, *The Dream of the Earth*, Sierra Club Books, 1990.

60. See Matthew Fox, *Original Blessing*, Bear & Co., 1989.

INDEX